Travel Well
The Gourmet Guide to Healthy Travel

by

Audrey Kaplan
&
Norman Kaplan, M.D.

Brontosaurus Press
3831 Turtle Creek, #20E
Dallas, TX 75219
214/528-9260

Essential Medical Information Systems, Inc.
P.O. Box 811124
Dallas, TX 75381

Published in the U.S. 1989

The suggestions provided in this book are not intended to replace the services of a health professional. Readers should consult with their own doctor before adopting the procedures in this book.

ISBN: 0-929249-06-5

Printed in the United States of America

Dedication

Our book is dedicated to the future well-being of the children of our issue:

Adam
Alex
Jayan
Sam
Sarah

along with any future supplements.

Acknowledgments

We wish to thank those who helped us put this book together:

- Dr. Anne P. Freeman and Dr. John P. Wells provided editing assistance
- Mr. Ronald Yock and Ms. Trina Richman provided the color illustration for the cover
- Sharon Washington and Susan Beaubien, secretarial assistance
- The food, travel and health editors/writers at the metropolitan newspapers and magazines who recommended many of the restaurants listed in Chapter 4
- All who have provided the knowledge to make traveling well both enjoyable and feasible

Foreword

Millions of people travel thousands of miles away from home every day.

Millions of people, concerned about their health, are changing their life styles, especially in relation to diet, drink and physical activity, so that they can reduce their risks of premature heart disease and cancer and can look and feel better.

The two groups of people overlap greatly in their concerns; for both traveling and changes in life styles are more common now among the affluent, the upwardly mobile, and the better educated. Obviously, there are millions of travelers who want to change their life styles, but traveling poses problems for them in maintaining their diets and those activity patterns which have become increasingly popular.

Hundreds of books have been written to help people change their life styles—particularly to lose weight—but such books are aimed primarily at "the home audience." And although there are hundreds of travel books, with a few exceptions, they do not relate to diet, to exercise, to stress, etc. Many books also describe restaurants in most of the major cities across the country, and although some of these books are concerned with "healthy eating," most of them feature only the "5-star" and the more up-scale restaurants.

To our knowledge, there are no books written for travelers that provide both the general health principles travelers need to know and the specific ways travelers can maintain their healthy life styles away from home.

This book will fill that need and will provide travelers with both the background principles and with the specific steps for staying healthy and enjoying life while they are on the road.

Be careful about reading health books. You may die of a misprint.—Mark Twain

Table of Contents

Why travelers (and those who stay at home) need to
change their life styles
Why traveling is a problem:
- more stress and guilt feelings
- less sleep and rest
- less healthy food
- too many temptations to stray
- fewer healthy choices

The latest scientific evidence in support of a more
healthful life style, designed to reach these goals:
1. Stop smoking, or at least smoke more safely
2. Lower your blood cholesterol
3. Keep your blood pressure down
4. Keep your weight near "ideal"
5. Reduce your susceptibility to cancer
6. Stay in good physical condition
7. Avoid unnecessary stress
8. Keep toxic substances out of your body

Solutions to the problems encountered during travel
Overcoming the fear of flying
Eating in-flight
Drinking and flying
Staying fit on board
Handling jet-lag
Problems with gas
Ozone
Motion sickness
Altitude sickness
Other discomforts of travel
Problems for those already sick
Problems for the disabled

Lists of hotels providing facilities for workout, jogging, and swimming, and of restaurants providing healthier menus in the forty largest cities in the U.S. and Canada. The cities are:

United States

Albuquerque/Sante Fe, NM
Atlanta, GA
Baltimore, MD
Boston, MA
Chicago, IL
Cincinnati, OH
Cleveland, OH
Dallas, TX
Denver, CO
Detroit, MI
Honolulu, HI
Houston, TX
Indianapolis, IN
Jacksonville, FL
Kansas City, MO
Las Vegas, NV
Los Angeles, CA
Louisville, KY
Memphis, TN
Miami, FL

Milwaukee, WI
Minneapolis/St. Paul, MN
Nashville, TN
New Orleans, LA
New York, NY
Oklahoma City, OK
Orange County and South, CA
Orlando, FL
Philadelphia, PA
Phoenix/Scottsdale, AZ
Pittsburgh, PA
Portland, OR
St. Louis, MO
Salt Lake City, UT
San Antonio, TX
San Diego/La Jolla, CA
San Francisco, CA
Seattle, WA
Tampa/St. Petersburg, FL
Washington, D.C.

Canada

Montreal
Ottawa

Toronto
Vancouver

Audrey's Observations

When a happy, reasonably healthy woman reaches definite adulthood (and I consider that to be forty-five and beyond), she asks herself a pertinent question: Now that the children are grown and off on their own, how do I get out of the kitchen? For me, the answer has been provided by some special circumstances.

I happen to be married to a teaching physician whose reputation permits him to speak wherever he wishes. In large measure, this is because of his wonderful ability to translate difficult medical information into easily understood material for the lay person.

We have always been mindful of cholesterol levels, salt, and certain oils in our everyday eating; however, we have never been able to say no to great gourmet dining. This all brings us to an afternoon lunch that was visible proof of heaven, at Le Bernardin in New York City. While we were enjoying this healthful cuisine, the idea came to mind of combining the latest and often the most poorly understood medical information into a guide to healthy gourmet restaurants. Our final touch was adding the names of hotels with workout facilities to keep the traveler's momentum going. The research, development, and writing of this book have provided me with the answer to my question: eating and living well on the road certainly keep me out of the kitchen.

About the Authors

Dr. Norman Kaplan is a physician, teacher, and communicator. He has been on the faculty of one of the nation's major medical schools for over twenty-five years, during which time he has done research in various aspects of endocrinology and cardiology, focusing for the last ten years on hypertension and the prevention of heart disease. In addition to caring for patients, he has lectured at almost every major medical center in the U.S. and he has visited most foreign countries. Dr. Kaplan has written twelve books and over 200 medical articles. His latest layman's book, *Prevent Your Heart Attack,* was published by Scribner's in 1982 and was reprinted in paperback by Pinnacle Press in 1984.

While continuing his teaching, clinical practice, and writing, Dr. Kaplan has done extensive television work. He was nominated for an Emmy award in 1986 for moderating the nationally acclaimed PBS series, "Here's to Your Health." The 1988-89 series, "Life Matters," which he moderates, promises to be another informative and well-received series.

Audrey Kaplan is a mother, a builder of homes, an art gallery owner and a venture capitalist—not necessarily in that order. When she travels with her husband, she tries to maintain, along with him, a reasonably healthy life style. Because cooking has never been one of Audrey's passions, this book was conceived to help her stay out of the kitchen. She subscribes to a philosophy of cooking suggested by Nora Ephron's mother: "If you worked hard and prospered, someone else would do it for you."

Preface

You have probably read a number of articles and books that promise:

- Weight loss without discomfort.
- Longer life with little effort.
- A more attractive, sensuous, and sexy you for only ten minutes of effort a day.

You have probably seen, bought, and maybe even read these recent best sellers:

- *Fit for Life* by Harvey and Marilyn Diamond.
- *Food for Healing* by Annemarie Colbin.
- *The Complete Scarsdale Medical Diet* by Dr. Herman Tarnower and S.S. Baker.

(Our reason for selecting these authors is that they are not only popular but are also often wrong, as we shall see.)

So, here you are, still overweight, worried about your blood pressure and cholesterol, dissatisfied with your diet and life style. You are not the trim, sexy person who will live happily ever after, as promised by these authors.

Why are you still the way you are, even if you have practiced what these authors have told you to do?

- First, these books (and most of what has been written) are often misleading, and sometimes, are just plain wrong.
- Second, being human, you simply cannot keep up with many of the weird expectations that the authors have included. (How many grapefruit can a person face in one week?)
- Third, knowledge about nutrition has grown considerably in the past few years. Unfortunately, however, many of the "experts" have not kept up, or never were well informed.
- Lastly, and most sadly, much of what you were promised—pounds dropping off while you could eat more and exercise less—simply were promises to get you to buy the book, not to help you achieve reasonable goals.

So, what's new? It has been this way since what was, probably, the first best seller of diet books in English *An Essay of Health and Long Life,* published in 1725 by the Englishman, Dr. George Cheyne, who settled upon a vegetarian diet with milk, tea, and coffee. During the ensuing 250 years, we have learned a great deal about health, but the promises of many authors have extended well beyond that knowledge. For example, here is what is promised in the "Foreword" to *Fit for Life*:

> *Fit for Life* is a breakthrough. No guilt, no burdens, no demands. Get healthy, thin, and vibrant very soon and determine your own pace. Rush down the freeway to health, or take your time to enjoy the last of the artificial flowers along the way - the chocolates, beer, pretzels, and porter-house steaks. It's all okay, Harvey and Marilyn Diamond tell us. Even the slightest change, the least little consistent effort, and healthy fitness ensues.

Consider: "No guilt, no burdens, no demands. Get healthy, thin and vibrant very soon. . . Even the *slightest* change, the *least* little consistent effort, and *healthy fitness ensues.*"

Who could resist? No wonder that, as the cover proclaims, it is "America's All-Time #1 Health and Diet book! Over three million copies in print!"

We think that you should resist those misleading promises (for a quick and easy fix) offered in *Fit for Life* and similar books which are written by poorly informed health gurus. A new diet book becomes a best seller about every three months, and most of these books offer misleading promises.

Our book is different. It will provide scientifically correct information with proven, practical advice on how to lose weight, how to lower your risks for heart disease, hypertension, and cancer, how to feel better, and how to live longer.

The process will not be too easy. Results will not come overnight. You will need will power and patience. However, we shall not demand that you abandon good sense, subject your stomach to strange diets, or inflict crazy practices upon your body.

We shall provide the best available, scientifically proven, and practical guidelines to help you get what you want—a slimmer figure, a healthier body, and a more positive attitude. Nothing we offer will be without scientific proof. Nothing we offer will be impractical for you to follow.

Benjamin Franklin has said it best in his *Poor Richard's Almanac*: "Wouldst thou enjoy a long life, a healthy body, and a vigorous mind, and be acquainted also with the wonderful works of God? Labour in the first place to bring thy appetite into subjection to reason."

We shall not be as strict as Franklin who also suggested: "The Difficulty lies in finding out an exact Measure; but eat for Necessity, not Pleasure, for Lust knows not where necessity ends."

We like pleasure and, even occasionally, a little lust. So read on. We offer you gourmet eating and a well-balanced program of dieting, of exercise, and of relaxation. It will be better than mother's chicken soup, with all its fat and salt and calories, and it should not hurt.

Chapter 1

Traveling Can Be Hazardous To Your Health

On any given day, millions of Americans are away from home, some for pleasure, others for business. Traveling, mostly by air, is obviously a necessary part of life for many of us. However, being away from home poses a number of problems that may impede our attempts to stay healthy or to improve our life styles. It is hard enough for people to control their weight, blood pressure, cholesterol level, exercise conditioning, and psychological equilibrium in the relatively stable home situation. On the road, it can be almost impossible.

Some of the reasons are obvious. Others, although of major importance, are not so obvious. For example:

MORE STRESS

Rushing to the airport and having to wait hours for a delayed flight (when there is only a little time before an important appointment in a distant city) are major stresses. Upon arrival, we are often thrown into a strange and hostile environment which may include New York cabs and Los Angeles freeways. Even worse may be a person's need to perform under adverse circumstances in giving a presentation to a client, in presenting a paper to a convention, or in closing a sale to a recalcitrant customer.

Being away from home may, in a subtle way, add to the psychological stress of travel. Because you are away from your spouse and the kids, you may feel guilty about relaxing and enjoying yourself. You take along extra work, even if you are not able to handle it as well when you are away from the office. To help relieve your guilt you carry bulging briefcases on the plane. Then, if the time and energy are not available during the trip, you bring the work home again adding further to your guilt.

LESS SLEEP AND REST

Even in a good hotel room, it is unlikely that you will sleep as soundly as you would at home—perhaps because you have had too much to drink on the plane or because you miss the comfort of your own bed and the warmth of your bed mate. Moreover, when you are on the road, you seldom have time for brief periods of rest and the longer periods for doing nothing, even for the relaxation of having lunch with friends or the occasions of dinner with your family.

LESS HEALTHY FOOD

You start with a meal on the plane (perhaps eggs and sausage for breakfast, meat and fattening assortments for lunch and, if you are really unlucky, a big steak for dinner). You will be eating completely different and much less healthful foods than you do at home. Your good efforts to eat right (with fewer calories and saturated fat, with more complex carbohydrates and fiber) appear to be sabotaged by travel, for varying reasons adding up to potent forces: too many sweet-rolls, too much booze, no "Lite Cuisine," no spouse to prepare and to share good home cooking, and too many fancy restaurants serving dishes that seem wonderful but are too high in calories, saturated fat, and protein. (After all, you certainly are not going to order a low calorie, low-fat meal at Lutece or Lawry's or at Ruth's Chris Steakhouse.) Then you add to the natural desire to relax with booze and food (to relieve the tensions of travel) the attitude that "a little indiscretion never hurts because I'll soon go back to my healthier usual life style." However, the "little indiscretions" take up half of your week, and you cannot undo the damage of four days of wicked eating, drinking, lack of exercise, and of high stress with a weekend of righteous living.

Never eat more than you can lift.—Miss Piggy

TOO MANY TEMPTATIONS TO STRAY

You often face one of two scenarios when you are away from home: feeling alone and bored or being with a gang of gregarious associates who want to live it up. Either way, you are tempted with lots of food and drink, and you have too little physical exercise (after all, it is dangerous to walk in the streets of most large cities at night). Ultimately, you find it hard to resist temptations without the order and comfort of your home. Perhaps, your lunch at home may be a bowl of soup and a diet drink; yet on the road it is a full meal. We do not smoke, but some of our friends tell us that they always seem to light up more on the road than at home.

FEWER HEALTHY CHOICES

At home you have considerable control over what you eat because you and your mate make the choices. Whoever does the cooking knows not only what you like but also what is good for you. And if you go out for dinner, you find that you go more and more to restaurants serving fish or to small ethnic restaurants serving Mediterranean-style food or Far Eastern delicacies, rather than fancy and rich haute cuisine or barbeque dripping with fat. However, on the road you are more likely to eat at your hotel or, if you are "unlucky," you dine at the best-known 5-star restaurant in town which probably features rich appetizers, juicy red meat that is 50% saturated fat, and heavy cream desserts that you "are to die for"—literally. The lesser known, and often healthier, restaurants remain unknown to most occasional travelers.

At home you may work out at the 'Y,' at a spa, or at a club. You may even jog round the neighborhood. On the road, however, facilities often are not available and, even if they are, you do not have the time for exercise. The breaks in the routine that occur when you are away from home often preclude your maintaining the level of physical exercise you achieve at home.

> *Great food is like great sex—the more you have, the more you want.*—Gael Greene

So, there you are, away from home, away from the routine of sleep and rest and physical exercise, away from the healthy eating and moderate drinking that a rapidly growing population of Americans are practicing. Notice the changes in food intake that have occurred in the U.S. over the past fifteen years (Table 1.1). These changes—to

TABLE 1.1: PER CAPITA CONSUMPTION, IN POUNDS

	1975	1984
Beef	119	106
Eggs (number)	276	261
Whole milk	178	133
Pork	55	66
Fish	12	14
Chicken	40	56

From *Statistical Abstract of the United States,* 1986.

avoid red meat that is high in saturated fat, to avoid high cholesterol eggs, and to consume more poultry and fish, fresh vegetables, and unsaturated fats—have been responsible for a significant fall in the average cholesterol level of the population. Changes in diet and the long-overdue reduction in the number of people who smoke cigarettes are mainly responsible for the major decline in deaths from heart attacks and strokes that has occurred in the U.S. since 1968 (Figure 1.1).

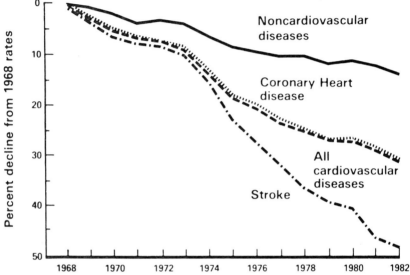

FIGURE 1.1 The percent change in deaths from noncardiovascular and cardiovascular causes in the U.S. from 1968 to 1982.

The downward curves seen in Figure 1.1 translate to over 500,000 Americans who are still alive and well, but who would be dead if they still ate and smoked as they did in the 1940s and 50s. Factors other than changes in diet and the cessation of smoking are also partly responsible, including better control of high blood pressure (hypertension) and, perhaps, increased levels of physical activity. However, according to the best analysis (1), the lower cholesterol induced by the change in diet and the reduction in cigarette smoking are the two major reasons behind this significant protection against serious cardiovascular disease.

While that is the good news, there is also bad news: cardiovascular diseases still are, by far, the leading cause of death in the U.S. Almost 1,000,000 people will die this year from heart disease and strokes, many of whom will be in their 40s, 50s and 60s. It is these premature, early deaths, striking down people in their prime, that give us most concern. Truthfully, we think that a quick and relatively painless heart attack at age eighty is a nice way to go. It certainly is better than a slow and painful death from cancer, which is by the way, going up at the same time deaths from heart disease are going down (Figure 1.2).

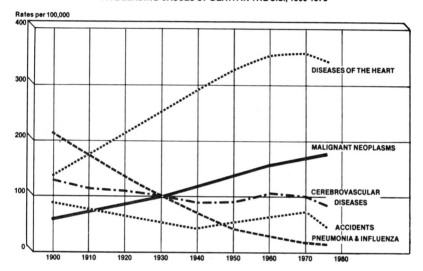

FIGURE 1.2 — The five leading causes of death in the U.S. from 1900 to 1976.

Two points to consider: both the rising deaths from cancer and the continuing high rate of premature deaths from heart diseases are largely preventable. At least one out of three cancer deaths is caused by diet and another third is caused by cigarette smoking (2). Further reductions in blood cholesterol, in high blood pressure, and in cigarette smoking could prevent the majority of premature deaths from heart diseases.

Obviously, we must do all we can to stay alive and healthy. However, as we have seen, traveling may be interfering with our best intentions. Those people who travel the most—the more affluent, the better educated, the more upwardly mobile—are also those who are concerned most with a healthier life style. The hard-won gains, unfortunately, may be lost by the excesses in food and drink, in the physical slow-down and in the psychological stresses that go with travel.

17

The territory, then, can be treacherous, and getting there may be the worst part of the trip. There are ways to avoid the traps. This book is written to be your guide to staying healthy when you are away from home. However, before we discuss the specific steps you should follow, we shall describe in the next chapter some general principles of good health and the latest scientific evidence in support of a healthy diet and life style, so that you will know why it is worth the trouble.

A word of caution: we do not promise you a longer life or phenomenal weight loss by "Immune Power," by "F factors," or by the nutritional quackery of *Fit for Life.* Most best-selling diet books promise impossible results through largely groundless, and often harmful practices.

We shall describe some major changes that you can make, particularly in your diet, that will improve your chances to stay alive and healthy, and if necessary, to lose weight and to look more attractive. Such helpful practices as increasing your intake of omega-3 fatty acids, cutting down on high protein foods, and drinking alcohol in moderation will be described in detail. We shall also give you specific suggestions on how to stay physically active and psychologically stable while you are away from home.

So read on. Armed with the facts provided in the next chapter, you will be given all of the details you need to follow a healthy life style while you are on the road.

Chapter 2
How To Stay Healthy Away From Home

Now that we have recognized the perils of travel, let us review the latest evidence about what can be done to stay healthy and to live longer. Our aim is to stay healthy until we reach a ripe old age, even if we spend a considerable amount of time on the road. We should not, however, have to suffer in order to gain a few extra years, particularly if we are asked to give up enjoyable features of an active life style in order to gain more time in an old-age home.

We shall ask nothing of you that is difficult to do (except to quit smoking) or for which an attractive alternative is not readily available. What we shall ask of you will not only add years to your life but also will add life to your years. It is possible to be away from home, and to do all of the positive things that contribute to good health, while you go about your business or pleasure. Eating well, staying fit, and keeping a relaxed attitude are possible even under adverse circumstances.

In the chapter that follows we shall list the places to eat and the places to stay that will make it possible for you to become even healthier away from home.

Goals for A Longer, Happier Life

Consider the most recent evidence about the major ways to stay healthy, so that you will understand better why proper diet, exercise, and relaxation are so important. The major ways to stay healthy are the following:

- Stop smoking, or at least smoke more safely.
- Lower your blood cholesterol.
- Keep your blood pressure down.
- Keep your weight at or just above "ideal."
- Reduce your susceptibility to cancer.
- Stay in good physical condition.
- Avoid unnecessary stress.
- Keep toxic substances out of your body.

Notice that weight reduction is not at the top of the list of health-promoting practices. The reason is that moderate obesity does not *in itself* pose much of a risk for premature heart disease or cancer. People who are significantly overweight do experience more disability and a higher death rate (3) (Figure 2.1), and most overweight people

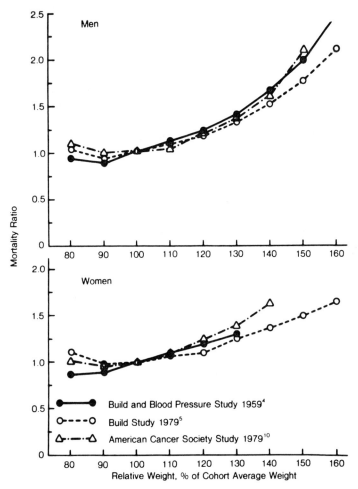

FIGURE 2.1: The relative mortality for men (top) and women (bottom) with increasing relative weight. (From Manson JE, Stampfer MJ, Hennekens CH, Willett WC. Body weight and longevity: a reassessment. JAMA 1987;257:353-358).

suffer psychological trauma as well. Obesity is a problem because of what frequently goes with it—high blood pressure, diabetes, and high blood cholesterol. These disorders more often accompany obesity that is distributed in the abdomen and upper body rather than in the buttocks, thighs, and lower body. If your extra weight is mainly in the lower part of your body, and if you are lucky enough to escape all of the problems that often accompany moderate obesity, you probably will not suffer medically. Of course, if you are grossly overweight, more than 100 pounds above your ideal, you will, most likely, suffer medically from various problems—including arthritis, sleep apnea, and inability to withstand surgery.

The grave doth gape for thee thrice wider than for other men.—William Shakespeare

Those people who are moderately overweight and who have high cholesterol, high blood pressure, or diabetes obviously must lose weight in order to overcome these serious problems. For those individuals who are only a few pounds overweight, and whose obesity is in the lower part of the body, weight reduction may be useful to avoid serious problems, but they should recognize the relatively benign nature of mild lower-body obesity and call it what it is: a social discomfort and not a medical disease.

Perhaps you have looked at the list of recommendations on the previous page and have said, "So, what's new?" The suggestions may seem to be ideas which everybody believes in and practices. If only that were so. Despite improvements made by a significant number of people, the truth is that a large number of Americans are still smoking, drinking and eating too much, exercising too little, and unnecessarily exposing themselves to risks.

The Current Situation

Here are some facts about what is happening in America today:

- The average life expectancy for both men and women is two to three years less than for people in many other industrialized countries (4). The Japanese are undercutting our car and computer industries and they are living longer to enjoy the profits.
- The average adult's weight has gone up almost five pounds in the last ten years, and the proportion of children who are overweight has increased more than 50% from 1963 to 1980 (5). More and more young people are becoming "couch potatoes."
- As the headline in the *New York Times* "Living" section reports: "Americans Are Returning to the Sweet Life." The percentage of people on diets fell to 19% from 27% over the last two years while their consumption of chocolate bars rose 46%.
- Consumption of beef, a major source of saturated fat which is on everyone's hit list, after declining from 88 pounds per capita in 1975 to 76 pounds in 1980, rose to 80 pounds in 1986 (6).
- The number of hypertensive people whose blood pressure is under good control is still a tiny minority of the total (7).
- Fifty-three million Americans continue to smoke and to light up 570 billion cigarettes a year, averaging well over 2,000 cigarettes per man, woman, and child in the U.S. (8).

21

We could go on and on citing statistics. The truth is simple: we Americans have got a long way to go to improve our life styles. In this book we address the extra problems introduced by traveling— obviously, a major part of the life of many Americans. Therefore, let us see how and why we can make some changes in our habits away from home.

The Burdens of Travel

As we have observed, just being away from home, and the social support that home provides, may make it more difficult for us to follow good health habits. At home the choices of food are often made for us and the opportunities for straying from a diet are fewer than when we are on the road. Usually, many of us eat well, exercise, and avoid risks because we want to satisfy the urgings of our family and friends, and without these urgings, we might lack the will power to persevere. Away from home, both the means and the motivations may be less available for us to keep on the straight and narrow path.

Sometimes, when a loved one announces that he has decided to go on a low-carbohydrate, low fat, low-salt diet, he is signaling that the middle (of marriage) is ending and the end is beginning.—Nora Ephron

You need to recognize that the strongest motivation to change must come from within. Unless you are convinced of the value of giving up bad habits and of taking on better ones, all of the support and coercion that come from home most likely will not work. It may be harder on the road to follow good health practices, but if you are convinced of the need to change, you can do it. We shall try to give you some useful suggestions.

Ways To Achieve The Goals

To achieve the eight primary goals, you will find a number of secondary means useful as ways of accomplishing what we have suggested. These include such matters as:

- Weight reduction
- A balanced diet with
  - reduced amounts of saturated fat
  - increased amounts of monounsaturated fat
  - increased amounts of omega-3 fatty acids

- reduced amounts of protein
- increased amounts of complex carbohydrates
- increased amounts of fiber
- Reduction in sodium intake along with increase in potassium
- Alcohol in moderation
- Regular isotonic exercise
- Relaxation and relief of stress
- Small amounts of aspirin (in selected populations)
- Avoidance of all unnecessary drugs and stimulants

We shall describe, in order, current knowledge about the importance of the eight major goals. As we proceed, we shall see how the secondary means can help you in reaching the primary goals.

Before we go into specific points, we shall consider a few general guidelines from behavioral psychology which may be helpful to you as you try to maintain a healthy life style while you are at home and away from home.

- Convince yourself of the need to make changes. Perhaps having a complete physical exam, or just a measurement of blood pressure and blood cholesterol, will show you why some changes are necessary. As we shall see, it is probable that you will have at least one problem that can and should be corrected.
- Knowing why you need to make some changes should not cause you unnecessary fear or anxiety. Although fear may be a powerful motive, your knowing that it is within your power to change should relieve your anxiety and encourage you to proceed.
- Realize that you can change. Millions of Americans—perhaps as many as thirty-seven million, have quit smoking (and there is no harder addiction than to nicotine).
- Feel good about what you do at the time you do it. You may reduce your cholesterol in order to prevent a heart attack in twenty years, but as you substitute fresh fruit and a crispy cereal for two eggs and three strips of bacon, you should relish the food now as a pleasurable taste sensation.

There is more simplicity in the man who eats caviar on impulse than in the man who eats Grapenuts on principle.—G.K. Chesterton

Accordingly, convince yourself that a temporary discomfort, if there is any, is worth the trouble for the reduction in risk that it brings.

- Decide how you will feel most comfortable in making some needed changes. Some people prefer to go whole-hog in straightening out ten bad habits at once. Other people find that approach uncomfortable and counterproductive. They prefer one step, even a small one, at a time, feeling more certain that eventually they will reach their goals.
- You may make changes to satisfy someone else, but you must recognize that your decision to change is a personal one for your own good—however much the changes benefit your children and the others who also depend upon you.
- Because the motivation to change must come from within, you should not depend mainly upon others to keep you on the straight and narrow path. You are the only person who will be around at the times of decision, and as a mature person, you will feel better in depending upon your own strengths. That is not to say that other people cannot and should not help you. Sometimes groups like Alcoholics Anonymous are absolutely essential. Frequently, a loving spouse can be supportive and should be asked to help in every way possible. Joint ventures with other people may even be more successful; it is hard enough to quit smoking without a spouse continuing to blow smoke your way.

Two of us liked dark meat and two of us liked light meat and together we made a chicken.—Nora Ephron

Now that we have looked at some general guidelines, let us review the eight major steps to a healthier life style, while we consider both the problems and the opportunities that occur during travel and being away from home.

STOP SMOKING

If you smoke cigarettes, stopping is the single most effective move you can make to become healthier, to live longer, and to reduce your risk for both heart disease and cancer. Because you certainly are well aware of this information, even if you have brain-washed yourself to deny the truth, there is little reason for us to try to motivate you to quit. We recognize the real psychological and physical attractions of smoking and the major trouble many people have in breaking the addiction. We can only encourage you to keep trying to quit and to use all the help that is available. As more is understood about the underlying mechanisms of addictions, better ways of breaking them are becoming available. Nicotine-gum is one of these ways. You can check with your doctor about it.

As a smoker or non-smoker, you encounter special situations when you travel:

• Non-smoking areas of airport lounges, restaurants, and hotels are being made increasingly available to go along with the non-smoking space on airplanes and the overall prohibition of smoking on flights that are less than two hours in duration. As non-smokers, we think that the non-smoking areas deserve to be kept as free of smoke as possible—a point that smokers seem increasingly willing to accept, even if they deny the physical harm of other people's smoke.

• More non-smoking areas should be made available in every space open to the public. Although smokers may be inconvenienced, we consider their inconvenience to be less than that suffered by non-smokers who have to breathe their second-hand smoke. Some people are willing to engage in major warfare to protect their respective spaces, but we hope that both groups will be tolerant: non-smokers of the need of addicts to get their fix and smokers of the need of others to stay free of noxious smoke.

We hope that our world can become smoke free before long. In the meantime, travelers need to encourage their carriers and their hosts to provide smoke-free space, particularly when they pay good money for its use. Just as some up-scale ski resorts provide bedroom humidifiers to alleviate the dryness of winter mountain air, perhaps room smoke filters can be provided for those travelers who are so sensitive that they suffer from the smoke left by previous inhabitants. And more hotels should provide non-smoking floors.

LOWER YOUR BLOOD CHOLESTEROL

You are hearing and reading more and more about the need to check your blood cholesterol, both the total and, if it is high, the HDL fraction. The reasons are multiple:

• The test is increasingly available and is easy to perform, requiring only a finger prick for obtaining a few drops of blood which can be analyzed on a portable machine in two minutes.

• The level of blood cholesterol is strongly related to the development of heart attacks and to other cardiovascular diseases, as shown by several surveys of middle-aged American men (9)

(Figure 2.2). However, the risk is lowered in the presence of a high HDL fraction which appears to be involved in transporting the bad form of cholesterol out of the blood vessels into the liver where it can be gotten rid of.

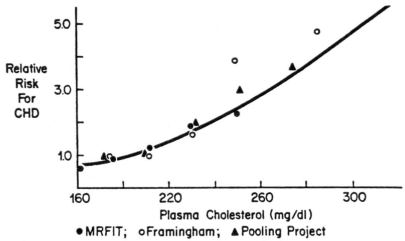

● MRFIT; o Framingham; ▲ Pooling Project

FIGURE 2.2 Relative risk for coronary heart disease (CHD) as a function of plasma cholesterol levels. In three epidemiologic studies, MRFIT, Framingham heart study, and the Pooling Project, the relation of levels of cholesterol to relative risk for CHD among American men aged 35 to 60 was positive, but the relation was curvilinear. (From Vega GL, Grundy SM. Treatment of primary moderate hypercholesterolemia with lovastatin (mevinolin) and colestipol. JAMA 1987;257:33-38).

- Lowering the level of total cholesterol has been shown to reduce the development of heart disease. It has even been possible to show, when blood cholesterol levels are lowered, an actual removal of some of the cholesterol-rich plaques which block blood vessels and which lead to heart attacks (10).
- Drugs have become available that are much more effective in lowering the blood cholesterol level (11). Although they will most likely become very popular, the best way to start the process is through a "prudent" diet, lower in saturated fats and cholesterol and higher in those fats that provide special protection—such as olive oil and omega-3 fatty acids.

A sound mind in a fat body slips around.—Richard Smith

Where You Are Now

Before you read about the dietary changes you should make, you should know that you probably have a cholesterol level that is too high and that you would be better off if it were lower. You should know what

26

your cholesterol level is, just as you should know what your blood pressure is. If you have not had a blood test for cholesterol done in the past few years, you should get one. The few dollars it will cost you are well worth the knowledge you will gain, that either you are protected against one of the three major risk factors for premature heart disease (along with cigarettes and high blood pressure), or that you need *to do something now* to reduce your risk.

The chances are that you will need to do something because the average cholesterol level for American men and women is above the level for maximum protection. In large surveys of adult Americans, the average blood cholesterol level is about 215 milligrams per 100 milliliters (mg/dL), meaning that half the number of people tested are above that level (12). Although that level, and the levels up to 250, used to be called "normal," we know now that what is average is now normal.

Where You Need to Be

Recall that the Japanese have a longer life expectancy than Americans. The Japanese also have a much lower rate of death from heart attacks—28 men per year per 100,000 in Japan versus 272 in the U.S., 7 women in Japan versus 67 in the U.S. There may be many reasons for their lower rate of death from heart disease, but one that surely is responsible is their lower blood cholesterol. As shown in Figure 2.3, surveys of healthy adults in Japan show their cholesterol levels to be considerably lower than ours in the U.S. Notice how closely related the cholesterol level is to the death rate from coronary heart disease in these various countries (Table 2.1).

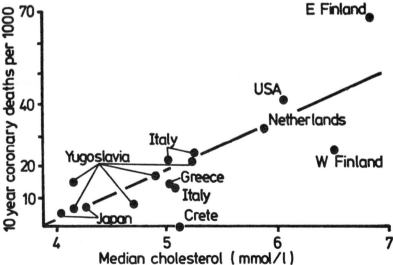

FIGURE 2.3: The 10-year-death rate per 1,000 from coronary disease in relation to the median cholesterol level in the populations of various countries. (From Truswell AS. Reducing the risk of coronary heart disease. Br Med J 1985;291:34).

TABLE 2.1
MORTALITY (PER 100,000) FROM CORONARY
HEART DISEASE AGE 45-54

Country	Men	Women
Finland	392	49
Scotland	353	79
England and Wales	272	50
USA	272	67
Sweden	160	26
Greece	102	14
Japan	28	7

The awareness of this close relationship between people in different countries and the similar, although less striking relationship within our own population of middle-aged men, shown in Figure 2.2, has led American authorities to recommend much lower cholesterol levels as the "ideal." The true ideal level appears to be well below 200, around 160. However, that may be asking too much of people, and so the consensus of a group of experts was to recommend through a proper diet that we aim for 200, if the level is between 200 and 240, and that we seek immediate attention if our levels are above 240, placing us at extra risk (13).

What is clear from Figure 2.2 is that the higher the cholesterol goes above the level of 160, the greater the risk is for a person to have coronary heart disease. Although we would all be better off with lower levels, medical attention is being directed mainly toward those individuals at higher risk. If your level is not above 200, you are at relatively low risk. Although there is a slightly lower chance of your developing heart disease if the cholesterol level is even lower, and some experts advocate levels as low as 160 to 180, our attitude is that the extra protection offered against heart disease by such low cholesterol levels is not worth the trouble it would take to get them that low. This consideration brings us to recommend 200 as the acceptable level.

Two weeks of the Scarsdale diet reduced my
cholesterol count to such a dangerously low level that I
had to get emergency transfusions of fat.—
Richard Smith

TABLE 2.2
THE CURRENT AND RECOMMENDED DIETS

	Current	**Recommended***
Total Cholesterol	500 mg/day	Below 300 mg/day
Total fat percentage of daily calories	40	below 30
Saturated fat: percentage of daily calories	15	below 10
Polyunsaturated fat: percentage of daily calories	6	below 10
Monounsaturated fat: percentage of daily calories	16	below 10
Polyunsaturated to saturated fat ratio:	4	more than 1

*Greater restrictions may be required for people with very high blood cholesterol levels.

If your total cholesterol level is above 240, indicating that you are at increased risk, you should change your diet *now* to reduce your level and to reduce your risk. Remember, however, that most of us would be better off with a lower cholesterol level, and that all of us, unless you already have a cholesterol well below 200, should change our diet from today's typical American diet to that recommended by the American Heart Association and most authorities in this field (Table 2.2).

As we shall see, the recommended diet is not that difficult to follow. It only asks for your prudence in staying away from high saturated (bad) fats and your increasing the intake of those fats that are beneficial. We think that everyone should follow this diet. If you do not need to, because your cholesterol level is already near or below the "ideal," you probably are already following such a diet. You may be protected by good genes or by luck, but it is quite likely that if you are safe from cholesterol, you are already engaging in safe eating.

With as much as we have heard about the need for safe sex, we should know that the need for safe eating is even greater. AIDS is terrible, and we are all appropriately concerned. But remember that heart attacks kill 100 times more Americans each year than AIDS. Unlike the situation with AIDS, we know that it is possible to overcome heart disease—by changing our diets in a way that will lower our cholesterol levels.

> *Gluttony is the source of all one's infirmities and the fountain of all our diseases. As a lamp is choked by a superabundance of oil, and a fire extinguished by excess of fuel, so is the natural health of the body destroyed by intemperate diet.—Richard Burton*

Some people argue that a change in diet is only needed for those who are at "high risk," saying that the rest of us can go on eating our current, relatively high fat, high cholesterol diet with impunity. We think that this approach is wrong. Let us use an analogy with AIDS to see why. Assume that a vaccine for AIDS will be discovered that will be highly effective in preventing the disease and that will be totally safe. Who will take the vaccine? Will the recipients be only the very high risk group of people who engage in promiscuous sex or in IV drug abuse? Of course not. Most of us will take the vaccine, even if our risk is very low.

The same situation applied to the last scary epidemic—polio. When Salk and Sabin had discovered a safe and effective vaccine, everyone rushed to take it, even though relatively few people were at high risk of developing the disease. It is obvious that, without knowing for sure who was susceptible, a lot more people needed to be protected than the relatively few who actually would develop the disease.

For heart attacks, the likelihood of your developing the disease is much greater than for AIDS today or polio back in the 1950s. Even though the prudent diet we recommend will not be as effective as a vaccine, it will reduce your risk, and so we think that all of us should follow it. This recommendation is based upon the certainty that what we recommend will not be harmful. Therefore, even if you do not need to change your diet, it will not hurt you to do so. That is obviously a fundamental requirement before any recommendation can be made for the public at large. The evidence for the safety of the type of diet we, and most authorities, recommend is uncontroversial. Not only are large populations following it—and have followed it for thousands of years—but also there has been no evidence of harm, a point indicated in careful studies of thousands of people who have changed to it. We are really trying to bring our diets closer to those followed by our ancestors, the type of diet that our body physiology was designed to handle, rather than the unnatural one we are now consuming (14) (Table 2.3).

TABLE 2.3
LATE PALEOLITHIC, CONTEMPORARY AMERICAN, AND CURRENTLY RECOMMENDED DAILY DIETARY COMPOSITION

	Late Paleolithic Diet	Contemporary American Diet	Current Recommendations
Total dietary energy (percent)			
Protein	33	12	12
Carbohydrate	46	45	58
Fat	21	42	30
Cholesterol (mg)	520	300-500	300
Fiber (g)	100-150	19.7	30-60
Sodium (mg)	690	2,300-6,900	1,100-3,300
Calcium (mg)	1,500-2,000	740	800-1,600

From: Eaton SB, Konner M, Shostak M. Am J Med 1988;84:739-49.

31

*Vegetarianism is harmless enough, though it is apt to
fill a man with wind and self-righteousness.—
Robert Hutchinson*

We do not say that there are no possible risks from going too far or
beyond the recommendations. Just as too much water can kill you, too
much of almost anything may be harmful. The prudent diet, however,
is not even potentially harmful, a fact based upon a substantial body of
strong evidence. Recall that when polio vaccines were first introduced, a few cases of polio developed because live virus got into
the original batches of vaccine. That situation led to an immediate
tightening of the manufacturing process, and since then, no further
trouble has been experienced. We have gone through a much longer
and a much wider testing of the prudent diet, so we need not be
worried about its potential for harm.

To carry the analogy one step further—the polio vaccine is easy
to take and one shot usually offers long-term immunity. So, once you
are protected, you can almost forget about the problem. Unfortunately, the prudent diet requires constant attention and more
active participation. However, as we shall see, the changes needed
are not that great, and there should be no more discomfort in following
the prudent diet than in taking a vaccine. Once you have accepted the
idea and you begin following the principles, the diet will become easy
and enjoyable. And, as you will see, we shall never ask you to say
"never." Sometimes, when there is no way out, bacon and eggs may
be the only breakfast available. But you should feel almost as concerned about such eating on a regular basis as you should about
unsafe sex. The consequences are even worse.

How to Change Your Diet

Now that you have seen why we all need to make some changes,
let us see what they are and how we can accomplish these changes at
home and on the road.

1. *Reduce saturated fat:* Saturated fats mostly come from animal
sources and are solid at room temperature. Palm oil and coconut oil
are obvious exceptions of fats of vegetable origin being mainly unsaturated (Figure 2.4). Watch out for them as the major ingredient in
most nondairy creamers and lots of snacks. Saturated fat is not only

FATTY ACID COMPOSITION OF OILS AND FATS

% of Total Fatty Acids

Saturated	Monounsaturated	Polyunsaturated

Safflower Oil

9	13	78

Sunflower Oil

11	20	69

Corn Oil

13	25	62

Olive Oil

14	77	9

Soybean Oil

15	24	61

Peanut Oil

18	48	34

Sockeye Salmon Oil

20	55	25

Cottonseed Oil

27	19	54

Lard

41	47	12

Palm Oil

51	39	10

Beef Tallow

52	44	4

Butterfat

66	30	4

Palm Kernel Oil

86	12	2

Coconut Oil

92	6	2

Sources: *Handbook No. 8–4* and Human Nutrition Information Service, U.S.D.A.

FIGURE 2.4: The fatty acid composition of oils and fats arranged by increasing percentage of saturated fatty acids (from Nutrition Action Healthletter, July-August, 1986).

more than two times higher in calories than protein or carbohydrate, but also much of it is converted in your body to cholesterol. Therefore you should:

* trim excess fat off meats
* eat lean meat, no more than three times a week
* choose fish, skinless chicken, and turkey over red meats (most shellfish is low in saturated fat and has no more cholesterol than lean meat or chicken, as seen in Table 2.4)
* boil, bake, steam, or roast foods instead of frying them
* choose skim milk products and lower-fat cheeses such as ricotta, mozzarella and farmer cheese
* use soft or light margarine made from polyunsaturated vegetable oils instead of butter

After the fall in beef consumption that followed the increasing awareness of the hazards of saturated fat, the beef industry has mounted a counterattack, spending $29 million in advertising in 1987. Their ads highlight the low cholesterol content of beef and the relatively small amount of saturated fat in three ounces of beef. That is true, but when was the last time you were satisfied with a three ounce steak? And, although it is true that beef (and most red meat) is relatively low in cholesterol, remember that it is the saturated fat we are concerned about. Recall that a really juicy marbled prime rib or sirloin may be forty percent saturated fat. That marbling may make the beef tender, but at the same time it is hardening your arteries.

TABLE 2.4
THE CHOLESTEROL CONTENT OF 3½ OUNCE PORTION OF COMMON FOODS FROM LOWEST TO HIGHEST

Food	Cholesterol (in milligrams)
Fruits, grains, vegetables	0
Scallops	45
Oysters	53
Clams	65
Fish, lean	65
Chicken/Turkey, light meat (without skin)	80
Lobster	85
Beef, lean	90
Chicken/Turkey, dark meat (without skin)	95
Crab	100
Shrimp	150
Egg yolk, one	270
Beef liver	440
Beef kidney	770

You may have heard that one of the major saturated fats in both beef and chocolate, stearic acid, has been shown not to raise cholesterol (15), but there are other saturated fats in beef that will.

There may be a way, however, of eating your beef and not getting large amounts of saturated fats. Most of the fat is in the beef because the cattle have been force-fed with fat-producing grain. While they stay penned up, they will not burn off any of it before they are slaughtered. Natural grass-fed, free-ranging cattle are being raised as a source of low-fat beef, such as those from the Red River Ranch near Dallas. You may find this kind of beef in your supermarket, but you should expect to pay a 20% or more premium for it.

In your travels away from home, however, you should expect to find much more saturated fat in your beef. The U.S. Grade AA Prime that most famous steak restaurants feature is graded that way because it has the highest fat content. Lower fat cuts are not considered to be tender and juicy enough for such places. It does seem inappropriate for the U.S. Department of Agriculture to classify the meat that is the worst for our health as the best for our consumption. But the Department has agreed to have the best lower fat cuts, formerly called only "Good," changed to the word "Select," a word which gives a much more positive connotation.

Meanwhile, the pork providers are touting their product as a safer alternative. In truth, pork has less saturated fat than beef, but most cuts have at least 10% fat, compared to 3.6% in chicken breast. So, Kosher chicken comes out better than non-Kosher pork with regard to fat as well. However, watch out: chicken fat, known as "schmaltz" by millions, is 29% saturated fat.

When a poor man eats a chicken, one of them is sick.—
"Fiddler on the Roof"

Fast Foods May Be Dangerous to Your Health

As bad as a Jewish mother's "schmaltz" may have been, what you get in most fast food emporia may be worse. Because they serve almost half of our out-of-the-home meals, you will certainly be tempted to get a quick, tasty and cheap lunch at one or another of them during your travels, particularly at the airport or on the highway. With yearly sales of over $50 billion a year, fast foods are here to stay.

The problem is that most fast foods are full of saturated fat. Hamburgers and French fries, even if cooked in vegetable oils, rather than in cheaper beef tallow, as they were until recently, add up to a lot of calories, sodium, and fat (Table 2.5). Fortunately, there are alternatives: "Roy Rogers Roast Beef" has less than 2% fat, compared to the 20% fat in a "Big Mac." Even better is the salad bar, or the tuna and coleslaw available in lots of sandwich shops and not-so-fast-food restaurants.

TABLE 2.5
TYPICAL FAST-FOOD LUNCH
VERSUS PRUDENT ALTERNATIVE

	Typical Fast-food meal: McDonald's "Big Mac", Regular fries, 12 ounce cola	A Prudent Alternative: Tuna sandwich with lettuce & tomato, coleslaw, fresh orange, iced tea
Total calories	927	415
Total fat, grams	45	12
Saturated fat, grams	19	3
Polyunsaturated fat, grams	10	5
Cholesterol, mg	95	48

2. *Reduce Cholesterol Intake:* As obvious as this seems to be as a way to lower your blood cholesterol level, the truth is that some people either do not absorb the preformed cholesterol that is in foods or, if they do, they reduce the production of their own cholesterol in the liver by an equal amount, so that their blood levels do not change if they ingest preformed cholesterol (16). However, there is no practical way to know if you are one of the lucky ones; so, the best advice is to cut the cholesterol content of your diet and hope that this will lower your blood cholesterol level. As shown in a recent study, if you are on a low saturated fat diet, with more polyunsaturated fatty acids and fiber-rich carbohydrate, you may not show a rise in blood cholesterol from as many as seven eggs a week (17). Nevertheless, the best advice is:

- Limit egg yolks to three a week (egg whites are no problem).
- Avoid organ meats—liver, brain, kidney, sweetbreads—which are the highest source of preformed cholesterol (Table 2.4).
- Limit processed lunchmeats, hot-dogs, and sausages which usually contain lots of saturated fat and cholesterol.
- Limit crab and shrimp which are higher in cholesterol than scallops, oysters, and clams.

More pasta and less panache.—Mario Puzo

In addition to diet, a number of drugs are now available to reduce blood cholesterol levels. Most of those drugs in use through mid-1987 were either difficult for people to take because of their bad taste or side effects, or they were only partially effective. With the availability of a new class of drugs that inhibit the action of an enzyme needed to make cholesterol, HMG-reductase (11), we have available a much easier to take and much more effective way to lower high cholesterol levels. The first of these, lovastatin (Mevacor), has been used mainly with one or another of the old-line agents to treat patients who have a genetic defect leading to markedly high cholesterol levels which cause heart attacks at a very young age. This drug and others of its class are being given to more patients with less markedly elevated cholesterol levels, and if these drugs continue to be both effective and safe, there will be a very strong temptation to use them in almost everyone who has any degree of high cholesterol.

Caution is advised, however. These drugs interfere with one of the body's basic systems because some cholesterol is an essential component of every cell in the body. Although they appear to be safe, they have only been tested in people for a relatively short time. Therefore, you should still use diet control as your first move in lowering your cholesterol. It may not be as sexy a way, or as easy a way, but it is certainly a safe way, and if you try, a reasonably effective way. If a prudent diet does not work, one or more of the lipid-lowering drugs may certainly be considered.

3. *Increase mono- and polyunsaturated fat,* particularly olive oil and fish oils containing omega-3 fatty acids. Unlike saturated fats, those that are unsaturated are mostly from vegetable (rather than animal sources) and are liquid rather than solid at room temperature. Unsaturated fats are not converted in the body into cholesterol. In fact, their consumption may lead to a decrease in cholesterol levels.

Until recently, most of the emphasis has been to increase polyunsaturates—the main fatty acids in safflower, sunflower, corn and soybean oils (see Figure 2.4). We have been encouraged to increase the proportion of polyunsaturated fat in the diet at the same time as we have been told to decrease the proportion of saturated fat, as shown in Table 2.2.

Hydrogenated Vegetable Oil

As you go through life's journey, you will come across many foods that contain polyunsaturated fats, fats made less unsaturated to create smoother tasting foods that are creamier and less likely to spoil. The process is called hydrogenation, meaning that hydrogen atoms have been inserted into the fats, saturating some of the unsaturated carbon bonds. Often the process converts the polyunsaturated into monounsaturate.

There is no major problem, particularly because, as we shall see, the monounsaturates contained in olive oil have suddenly become nature's little darlings. Yet, there may be some problem because there is a subtle difference between the natural monounsaturates, such as those found in olive oil, and the manufactured monounsaturates, found in margarine or in cooking shortening. It involves the position of the hydrogen atoms, trans in the manufactured versus cis in the natural. That is mainly of interest to chemists, but we are not quite as sure about the long-term safety of the trans-forms, as we are about the cis-forms.

In the meantime, many processed foods contain "partially hydrogenated vegetable oil" and there is little you can do to avoid them, particularly in restaurants where you have no idea of what is in many of the dishes. It may be yet another reason to eat more fresh natural foods which, if they are cooked, should not be fried.

Two New Players

In the recent past, two new players have been put into the game, both having been on the sidelines for thousands of years and having provided protection for millions of people without our knowing about their extraordinary capability. One, olive oil, is probably the main reason for those who consume the typical Mediterranean diet having much less heart disease, even though their total fat consumption is as high or higher than ours. The other, omega-3 fatty acid, may be the reason that Eskimos, and others who eat lots of cold-water fish, hardly ever have a heart attack.

So, as of now, the perfect dish would appear to be sardines packed in olive oil. The main drawback is the number of calories: 460

in one 3.75 ounce tin of the Crown Prince brand of tiny brisling Norwegian sardines in pure olive oil. There are 450 milligrams of sodium in that little tin. You can also get considerable amounts of omega-3 fatty acid from other fishes more likely to be found in restaurants (Table 2.6) (18), and there are lots of ways to get extra olive oil into your diet.

The scientific rationale behind the current enthusiasm for both olive oil and omega-3 fatty acids goes beyond their effects on blood cholesterol. Because their major advantages are different, let us look at each in more detail.

TABLE 2.6
OMEGA-3 FATTY ACID CONTENT AND CALORIE
CONTENT PER 4 OZ. SERVING

Fish	Omega-3 Fatty acids (in grams)	Calories
Sardines, in fish oil	5.83	278
Salmon, pink	2.51	142
Tuna, albacore	2.40	197
Mackerel, Atlantic	2.17	201
Trout, lake	1.60	185
Halibut, Atlantic	1.49	131
Swordfish	1.03	139
Bass, striped sea	0.80	107
Snapper, red	0.69	126
Oysters, American	0.58	85
Mussels	0.49	91
Flounder	0.34	103
Clams, hard shell	0.27	62
Shrimp	0.23	104
Perch, lake	0.23	98
Haddock	0.23	95
Cod	0.23	86
Scallops, sea	0.21	99
Sole	0.11	101
Lobster	0.07	106

Olive Oil—The Real Power Behind Popeye

For thousands of years, at least as early as 6000 B.C., olive trees have been cultivated and olive oil has been used as a major ingredient in the diets of people in the area surrounding the Mediterranean Sea. Would you believe that there are thirty kinds of olives grown in Greece, and not one of them with pimento? Ten or so are imported into the U.S., including dark purple Kalamatas and Amfissas, black Thasos, green Naplion, Ionian and Atalanti.

Except the vine, there is no plant which bears a fruit of as great an importance as the olive.—Pliny, 79 B.C.

Although their names sound exotic, their oils are more important. We find some interesting connotations in the epithets for the oils. There is a "pure," a "virgin," and (would you believe) an "extra virgin" to choose from. As you might imagine, "extra virgin" is the rarest and most expensive oil. These terms indicate the amount of impurities, lending a different flavor, color, and aroma to the oils. However, we are really concerned with the basic olive oil, containing 77% monounsaturated fat, only 9% polyunsaturated and 14% saturated.

Those who consume lots of olive oil, and it is the source of as much as three-fourths of the total fat content in many traditional Greek diets, have been found to have fewer heart attacks as well as less cancer. There may be multiple reasons for the better health of Greeks, but a major one appears to be the consumption of olive oil.

Over the last few years nutritional experts, including Dr. Scott Grundy at our medical school in Dallas (19), have carefully examined the effects of monounsaturated fats, including olive oil, on blood cholesterol, both the bad form and the good HDL fraction. Surprisingly, the total cholesterol and bad forms were reduced, and even more surprisingly, the good HDL fraction was not. The first surprise came from the realization that monounsaturates could lower the total cholesterol as much as polyunsaturates. The greater surprise was the recognition that with polyunsaturates the level of good HDL-cholesterol fell—whereas, with monounsaturates, the HDL fraction stayed the same or even rose (20) (Figure 2.5).

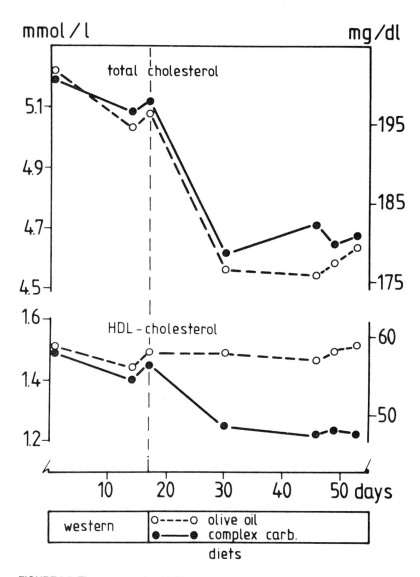

FIGURE 2.5: The serum total and HDL cholesterol in 48 subjects who first ate a diet high in saturated fat for 17 days. Then half received an olive oil rich diet, the other half a diet low in fat and high in complex carbohydrates for 36 days. (From Mensink RP, Katan MB. Effect of monounsaturated fatty acids versus complex carbohydrates on high-density lipoproteins in healthy men and women. Lancet 1987;1:122-124).

The information shown in Figure 2.5 shows the changes in total cholesterol and HDL-cholesterol fraction when 48 normal people were switched from our typical high saturated fat diets (Western) to either a diet enriched with olive oil or to a diet enriched with complex carbohydrates (bread, potatoes, fruits, and vegetables). As you can see, both enriched diets, with less saturated fat, caused the total cholesterol to fall. With the extra complex carbohydrates, the good HDL fraction also fell, but with the olive oil, the HDL fraction actually rose a slight amount.

The extra olive oil in this study was given in the form of a special bread, but the oil amounted to only about three teaspoonfuls which could be added in various ways.

Dr. Grundy who knows a great deal about the relations between diet and heart disease says, "In the fight against heart disease, olive oil may be a better weapon than the popular polyunsaturates like corn oil and safflower oil" (21). So, what Greeks and Italians have been doing for thousands of years, wholly unaware of what the olive oil was doing to their HDL levels, was protecting them against heart disease. As another benefit, their olive oil-rich diet appears to protect them against intestinal cancer as well (22). The only spoiler is that, like all fats, olive oil is calorie rich, nine calories to the gram, unlike the four calories in a gram of carbohydrate. However, if you substitute olive oil for other fats, such as the safflower oil you have been putting on salads or the corn oil you have been cooking with, you will not add to your caloric load.

Good oil, like good wine, is a gift of the gods. The grape and the olive are among the priceless bene-factors of the soil, and were destined, each in its way, to promote the welfare of man.—George Ellwanger, 1903

Omega-3 Fatty Acids—Fishing for Health

Already you may be taking capsules of concentrated fish oil containing almost pure omega-3 fatty acids, because about $200 million of them have been sold in 1987. Almost certainly you are eating more fish, because per capita seafood consumption in the U.S. has risen from about ten pounds in 1961 to over fifteen pounds in 1986, with projections that it will rise to thirty pounds by 1990 (23). The fish business took in $16 billion in 1986, more than the $12 billion in (cheaper) chicken, but still far below the $44 billion for beef. You will find fish featured increasingly both in haute cuisine restaurants and in fast-food emporia.

The main reason for the increased consumption of fish is that it has been touted as a healthier substitute for red meat. As a result, fresh fish is easier to find both in supermarkets and in restaurants. The consumption of fish will continue to rise because of the increasing evidence that extra health benefits are gained from the major oils in fish, which go by the tongue-twisting names of eicosapentaenoic acid (EPA) and docohexaenoic acid (DHA). Because both have a double-bond (site of unsaturation) at the third carbon position, they are called omega-3 fatty acids.

By whatever name, these fish oils appear to be good for us. As with olive oil, the best evidence comes from the people who have been eating fish long before we (or they) knew it was healthy. Groups such as Eskimos in Greenland, fishermen in Japan, and Indians in the Pacific Northwest have always eaten lots of fish, and they rarely die of heart attacks. They have been found also to have lower levels of bad total and LDL-cholesterol and higher levels of good HDL-cholesterol than the neighboring people who eat less fish. It has now been shown that the more people eat fish, the lower their risk is of dying from heart disease. In a study from Holland, involving 850 men observed for twenty years, those who ate at least an average of one ounce of fish a day were 2.5 times less likely to die from heart disease than men who ate no fish at all, even though the total fat intake of those who ate fish was higher (24).

The major beneficial ingredient in fish is now thought to be their omega-3 fatty acids, which as seen in Table 2.6, are found in largest amounts in cold water fish which, presumably, need more fat to keep them warm. These omega-3 fatty acids have been given to people with high cholesterol levels, and the cholesterol levels have been found to come down; in one study from an average of 373 to 207 milligrams per 100 millimeters of blood (25). However, in other studies involving diabetic patients, cholesterol levels have risen, so the effect of omega-3 fatty acids on blood lipid levels needs further study.

Nevertheless, these omega-3 fatty acids have been found to have other beneficial effects—preventing the clotting of blood, relieving arthritis, and lowering blood pressure. You may rightfully wonder about these disparate effects. The most likely explanation is that they increase the levels of some natural hormones, called prostaglandins, which may affect these various body functions.

For now, however, the omega-3-fatty acids are mainly being touted for prevention of heart attacks because of their effects on cholesterol, and, possibly, because of their effects on blood clotting as well. Because man is an inherently lazy species who does not want to catch his fish every day, and because entrepreneurs abound, the omega-3 fatty acids have been squeezed out of fish and put into capsules, each providing 300 to 500 milligrams, less than one-fifth of that in a four-ounce portion of pink salmon. These fish oil supplements, if two are taken each day, will set you back $7 to $15 per month. That is a lot less than the cost of fish at LeBernardin, but there is no evidence that these supplements will, in fact, reduce your risk for heart disease. As we shall see, you can get the effect of these fish oil supplements on cholesterol by using more olive oil and other unsaturated fats, and the effect on blood clotting by taking an aspirin every other day. Most authorities, including the American Heart Association, continue to advise caution in the use of fish-oil capsules.

For now, we think it is a lot more fun to eat more fish. But, if you want to supplement your diet with the fish-oil capsules, it is unlikely that you will be harming yourself, and there is a chance that you will improve your health.

By the way, avoid too much of another rich source of omega-3 fatty acid—cod-liver oil. Along with the fatty acids, it is loaded with enough Vitamins A and D to cause serious overload and toxicity. Mother may have had a good idea in getting a teaspoon down our throats to give us the vitamins, but more than that for obtaining omega-3 fatty acids could lead to trouble.

Those who cannot or who will not eat fish and prefer to await evidence about the long-term value and safety of the fish-oil capsules may obtain omega-3 fatty acids, of a somewhat different form, from some plants, including purslane, soybeans, walnuts, and butternuts. Other sources include wheat germ oil, rapeseed oil, and tofu.

For most of us, fresh fish seems to be more accessible. You will find lots of Japanese restaurants serving sushi and sashimi in the lists in Chapter 4. Obviously, raw fish is another excellent source of omega-3 fatty acids.

Raising the HDL

You should do everything possible to raise and not to lower your HDL-cholesterol fraction at the same time as you lower your total cholesterol. This includes limiting polyunsaturates and—as seen in Figure 2.5—complex carbohydrates. There are three other things you can do to raise your HDL fraction:

- exercise fairly vigorously
- drink small amounts of alcohol
- if you are a postmenopausal woman, take estrogens

One can say that the way to live longer is to be a woman on estrogens who jogs to the liquor store each day.

We shall examine the beneficial effects of exercise and moderate alcohol consumption later in this chapter.

KEEP YOUR BLOOD PRESSURE DOWN

Some of the changes that will lower your blood cholesterol may also help to keep your blood pressure down. Claims have been made for omega-3 fatty acids and a low saturated fat intake. However, more certain reduction of high blood pressure—a need for the forty million Americans who have hypertension—can be provided by weight reduction, restriction of sodium, and moderation in the use of alcohol (26). Some other ways, in addition to the various antihypertensive drugs, may also help, including increased amounts of potassium, exercise, relaxation, and the relief of stress.

In view of the possibility that your blood pressure may already be up, or at least, may need to be kept from going up, let us look at various non-drug ways to lower your pressure. If these do not work, or if your pressure remains too high in spite of them, varieties of effective drugs are available, so that almost everyone can be treated successfully for high blood pressure.

Restriction of Sodium

Sodium is the main mineral in your blood fluids. If your body has too much sodium, your blood vessels become filled excessively, subsequently raising your blood pressure. Hypertension is related to many factors, but too much sodium within the body is almost certainly one of the major causes. Although most people who consume high levels of sodium will not develop hypertension, if you are genetically predisposed, your body may not be able to handle the extra sodium that almost all of us ingest.

You are probably getting much more sodium than you need, mainly in the form of table salt or sodium chloride, at an average of 12,000 milligrams (mg), or three teaspoonsful a day. Most of the sodium does not come from what you add at the table or from what the person who has cooked your meal has added in the kitchen. Most of the sodium is "hidden" sodium that is added in the processing of almost every canned, precooked, or prepared food you eat. It is "hidden" because, unless you look on the label of the forty percent of foods that have the sodium content listed, you would never know it was there. Does a little can of tomato juice taste as if it has almost

45

one-third of the recommended total day's sodium, almost a half of a teaspoonful of sodium chloride in one six-ounce glass? Look at the label: 650 mg. of sodium or 1.5 grams of sodium chloride in a small can (sodium is forty percent of sodium chloride).

Unless you try unsalted tomato juice, which tastes terrible, you would never realize there is any sodium in what you drink. Another example: there is more sodium in an ounce of Corn Flakes than in an ounce of potato chips. Some other examples are shown in Table 2.7.

TABLE 2.7
THE SODIUM CONTENT OF SOME COMMON FOODS
(1000 mg Sodium = 44 mEq Sodium)

Comparable foods with either low or high sodium content

Low

Shredded Wheat:	1 mg/oz
Green Beans, fresh:	5 mg/cup
Orange Juice:	2 mg/cup
Turkey, roasted:	70 mg/3-oz
Ground Beef:	57 mg/3-oz
Pork, uncooked:	65 mg/3-oz

High

Corn Flakes:	305 mg/oz
Green Beans, canned:	925 mg/cup
Tomato Juice:	640 mg/cup
Turkey dinner:	1,735 mg
Frankfurter, beef:	425 mg each
Bacon, uncooked:	1,400 mg/3-oz

Sodium content of some "Fast Foods"

Kentucky Fried Chicken (three pieces of chicken, potatoes, gravy, coleslaw and roll)	2,285 mg
McDonald's Big Mac	962 mg
Burger King Whopper	909 mg
Dairy Queen Chili Dog	939 mg
Taco Bell Enchirito	1,175 mg

Some foods with very high sodium content

Catsup, one tablespoon:	156 mg
Olive, one:	165 mg
Cinnamon roll, one:	630 mg
Soup (chicken noodle), one cup:	1,050 mg
Dill pickle, one large:	1,928 mg

Because most of the sodium you get is in processed foods, you have an opportunity to get less when you eat out at restaurants that prepare your food from scratch. Just ask the waiter to have the salt left out in the cooking. The less expensive the restaurant and the faster the food is prepared, the less chance you have of keeping out the sodium. "Big Macs" come presalted with about 950 mg. of sodium and, even more than with the beef, there is no way to cut the salt. The least salted food at McDonald's is the French fries, unless you use ketchup which adds almost 200 mg. of sodium per tablespoon.

There are some other salt mines. The MSG in many Chinese restaurant dishes is monosodium glutamate. Alka-Seltzer is almost pure sodium bicarbonate. A major preservative in processed meats is sodium benzoate. The list goes on and on, except in natural food. Nothing that comes out of the ground—fruits or vegetables—and nothing that grows on natural food—fish, poultry, or cattle—have any significant amount of sodium in them. That should give us a message: the human body is designed to handle a low-sodium diet because that is what our ancestors took in during the thousands of years our species was evolving (see Table 2.3). The large amount of sodium we are now taking is unnatural. Therefore, there is no danger and, potentially, a great deal of good to be gained from cutting it down.

We are not suggesting a very low sodium intake. That is impractical these days unless you are eating completely natural foods. And, like tomato juice, there are some foods that just need some sodium to make them palatable. But here is what you can do to cut your sodium intake by half—to a level of about 2,000 mg. a day, or 5,000 mg. of sodium chloride:

- Do not add salt at the table; use other spices and seasonings, but not soy sauce, sea salt, or any other "salt."
- Cut down or cut out salt added in cooking. Ask that your food be prepared with little or no salt and that sauces be served on the side. It is usually helpful to order the simplest foods on the menu such as broiled fish or grilled chicken. Be aware that many of those fabulous sauces that make cuisine so haute are prepared hours ahead, and you may not get such dishes cooked to order without salt. Remember, however, that you are paying for what you eat, and the more expensive the restaurant is, the greater the possibility you will be able to eliminate the salt as well as the butter, eggs, and fat if you ask.
- Stay away from heavily salted foods such as pickles, corned beef, and sauerkraut.

- Limit your intake of "hidden" salt, which may be less of a problem on the road than at home, but a problem wherever you eat processed foods.
- Watch out for fast foods, pickled vegetables and meats, and heavily salted cheeses.

Pepper is small in quantity and great in virtue.—Plato

Be prepared for a bit of a taste letdown at first. A palate that has been overwhelmed by sodium for forty years may need some time to get used to less. However, you will soon be surprised by how much better and how much more interesting many foods will taste without as much sodium. After the initial shock, most people quickly adjust to preferring less sodium. You will wonder how you ever loved mother's chicken soup.

Other Ways to Lower Your Blood Pressure

Extra body weight, too little exercise, too much stress, too little potassium, and too much alcohol are other factors that may raise your blood pressure. To lower your pressure, try these suggestions:

- Weight reduction: even a few pounds may make a difference. You may literally cure your hypertension if you take off enough weight.
- Exercise: regular isotonic (aerobic) exercise may lower your pressure, probably by dampening the activity of your automatic (autonomic) nervous system that tends to keep your blood vessels tightened.
- Relaxation: any form of relaxation, from TM to biofeedback to yoga, has worked for some of its practitioners.
- Increasing potassium: just the reverse of sodium, our bodies are getting much less potassium than during previous times. Natural foods are much richer in potassium, most of which is leached out during processing.
- Moderation in alcohol: more than four drinks a day probably will raise your blood pressure. As we shall see, one or two drinks a day are quite likely to be good for you, but when you go much beyond, you are asking for all sorts of trouble, hypertension being one of the major difficulties.

A Few Words About Medications

For most people with persistently high pressures above 140/90 who do not respond adequately to the various non-drug therapies, one or more antihypertensive drugs will be needed to bring the pressure down to a safer level. Over forty different medications are available today and the number keeps growing as more effective and less bothersome drugs are introduced.

The three major types of antihypertensive drugs are: diuretics, sympathetic nervous system blockers, and vasodilators, with a number of sub-divisions under each major type. One or another may be most appropriate for each hypertensive person, and sometimes multiple attempts must be made before the most suitable drug is found. Do not be discouraged—for the right drug or combination of drugs can almost always be found which will lower your pressure and will not cause side effects. Newer agents, such as alpha-blockers, ACE inhibitors, and calcium blockers are replacing some of the older choices such as diuretics and beta-blockers. In view of our desire to keep your cholesterol down and to encourage your doing lots of physical exercise, we think that one of the alpha-blocker group is a particularly attractive choice for many people because these agents tend to have no adverse effect on cholesterol and not to limit the heart's response during exercise.

KEEP YOUR WEIGHT NEAR "IDEAL"

Many of us do not have to lose weight, but we probably want to anyway. If you are five, ten, up to twenty pounds above the "ideal," you are overweight and that is, most likely, only a social problem. If you are heavier, around twenty extra pounds for most women, thirty to forty pounds for most men, you are obese, and that is liable to pose some health hazards as well. However, for those of us, mainly middle-aged men who have shifted our weight more and more into the abdomen and upper body, even a little obesity can be a major threat to health.

Imprisoned in every fat man a thin one is wildly signalling to be let out.—Cyril Connolly, 1945

Even for those of us who are only slightly overweight, those extra few pounds can present a major psychological burden, even if they do not harm our health. In fact, our attempts to shed those extra few pounds may be more of a health hazard than the weight itself. Witness the epidemic of bulimia and anorexia among high school and college girls. Take heart, however, for the fashion model look of the 70s, with models appearing svelte and thin, flat-chested, and with no hips, is giving way to their having some curves, a soft and rounded look, with even a few muscles. Therefore, there will be less pressure, we hope, on young women to flagellate their bodies unnecessarily to achieve a mystical, perfect look for the times.

The problem faced by those of us who are only a few pounds overweight is primarily one of perception, not so much the way others perceive us, as the way we perceive ourselves. And while we do not underrate the strength of even false perceptions, we both perceived the five to ten pounds of extra weight, which we used to carry, provided us with sufficient motivation to begin a regular exercise program. We also reduced our caloric intake until those pounds were shed. We consider this attitude to be reasonable, even if it uses the false perception of being overweight as its motivation. To go through some gentle deprivations and healthful practices is good sense. To go through major and abrupt upheavals, however, such as spending weeks and thousands of dollars in a health spa (more like boot camp) or to purge and to vomit every morsel of food consumed, obviously, is foolish and is often extremely harmful.

Look back at Figure 2.1. Although the lowest death rate was found at a weight about 10% below average, the ratio of excess mortality really rises very little until you are more than 20% over the average weight. There is also considerable evidence that excess weight around the hips is not as much of a health problem as the weight around the middle (27). So, if you have become a "pear," you need not worry as much as if you have become an "apple." Those individuals who have experienced a steady increase in waist size, and that includes a considerable portion of American men over age thirty-five, have an increased chance of developing hypertension, diabetes, and high blood lipids, conditions which can increase the risk of heart attacks. That abdominal fat is metabolically very active, releasing lots of fatty acids which go into the liver and which, in a rather complicated way, lead to high levels of insulin in the blood. The combination of high levels of fatty acids and insulin appears to be responsible for a rise in blood pressure, for the development of diabetes, and for high blood triglyceride levels. So, if our weight has shifted to the middle, even if the total weight has not gone up much, do what you can to get rid of that "pot belly."

Our major message to the large number of individuals—up to half of 45 to 54-year-olds in the United States who are only slightly overweight—is to take it easy. There are sensible ways to shed those extra few pounds, in a gradual and comfortable manner, and to keep them off.

For the others, making up about thirty-five million Americans who are obese with 20% or more weight above the "ideal," we have got a bigger, more immediate problem. That much excess weight, particularly if it is in the middle and upper parts of the body, may pose a serious risk to your health. If you do not start losing it, you will, most likely, suffer physical consequences, along with the emotional trauma that comes from being fat in a world that simply does not like fat people.

Nobody loves a fat man.—Fatty Arbuckle, 1907

We offer two disclaimers about the previous paragraph. First, the health risks from obesity, as serious as they are in the long run, are usually not immediate, and some people who are quite obese may escape them. Second, although some obese people are emotionally secure and happy, we wonder if they should be. We are aware of efforts to enhance the self-esteem of obese people. Yet, as much as we think that all of us should feel good about ourselves, we also regard much of the effort to help obese people to be happy and content with their current states, as a manifestation of the major problem behind a great deal of true obesity—that is, deception. Fat people may deceive themselves in these various ways:

- "It's not what I eat, it's my metabolism." As in most deceptions, there is some truth in the statement. Many fat people have slower rates of metabolism, and they burn fewer calories during their ordinary life activities. However, that condition makes their need to reduce caloric intake even more critical.
- "I already eat less than a bird." Again some truth appears, although a sarcastic response might be, "Sure, like a vulture." Because of the lesser burning of calories or the more efficient metabolism, some people need fewer calories to maintain or to gain weight. But no one, nowhere, disobeys the laws of thermodynamics: weight will be gained when, and only when, caloric intake is above caloric expenditure. When the intake is reduced below expenditure, weight will, just as surely, be lost.
- "I can only lose weight for the first few weeks on a diet." This statement is true enough, for usually two reasons: first, much of the initial weight loss is fluid, not fat, and the extra fluid is only lost at the beginning of the diet; second, most people simply will not or cannot continue to follow the crazy diets they start with such enthusiasm.

Even more deceptions exist, including: most fat people are happy and content with themselves. We certainly do not want those people who are fat to be unhappy and depressed. However, we think that their acceptance of obesity as "the only way they can be" or, even worse, as "the way they would rather be" is deceptive and is potentially dangerous. Being obese is simply an uncomfortable and unhealthy condition. Therefore, we say: be happy but keep trying. You can lose weight and it is worth the effort.

Wouldst thou enjoy a long life, a healthy body, and a vigorous mind, and be acquainted also with the wonderful works of God? Labour in the first place to bring thy appetite into subjection to Reason.—Ben Franklin's Poor Richards Almanac

How to Lose Weight on the Road

The extra caloric temptations and the lesser chance for physical exercise while you are away from home, may make it nearly impossible for you to lose weight while you are on the road. Perhaps we should be realistic in only trying to keep any extra weight off and in leaving the stricter diets for home.

Yet, that is a cop-out and a put-down for the time we spend at home. After all, home should be as much fun and pleasure as travel is, particularly when the travel is to Omaha!

Always leave something on the table, especially if others are still eating.—Richard Smith

Let us consider what can be done on the road:

- On the way, avoid vending machines and fried foods at the airport. (A list of healthier menus that are available on the major U.S. airlines is given in the next chapter.)
- Don't start off feeling famished: working through lunch may be necessary, but you should try to eat some low-caloric vegies or snacks before you go out to dinner.
- Choose your restaurant: traditional French haute cuisine is inevitably high calorie, high fat, high salt, and who knows what else. Nouvelle cuisine, which is more often available, usually offers less of all the bad and plenty of the good aspects. Seafood, in Japanese or in traditional Italian and Greek restaurants, will be a

lot easier on your heart and blood vessels than the steak houses that offer sixteen-ounce "Prime" sirloins and little else. (In Chapter 4, we shall provide you with a list of some suitable restaurants in every major U.S. city.)

- Be assertive: you are paying for what you get, so get what you want. If you do not find the type of dish you want on the menu, ask the waiter if you can get a low-fat meal, such as grilled fish or chicken. If what you get is not what you have ordered, send it back.
- Ask for sauces and dressings on the side so that you can control how much you put on the salad or the dish.

> *To make a good salad is to be a brilliant diplomatist - the problem is entirely the same in both cases. To know how much oil one must mix with one's vinegar.—Oscar Wilde*

- Make your own salad dressing of vinegar and olive oil.
- Drink alcohol slowly and easily: a white-wine spritzer or a light beer will fill you up a bit, but it will not add many calories. Limit your total alcohol intake to two or three drinks, both to stay sober and to enjoy more the taste of your food.
- Start your meal with a low-calorie, filling soup or with a large salad.
- Consider having an appetizer as a main dish.
- Share an entrée with a dinner companion.
- Leave some food on your plate. Perhaps you were taught as a child to be a "clean-plate commando" and warned about the "starving Armenians," but it is no sin to quit before you are stuffed. Doggie bags are available if you are willing to use the leftovers for tomorrow's lunch.
- When you are nearly full, ask the waiter to take your plate. Even before then, you might ask that no more than one round of rolls be put on the table.
- Eat your favorite food first, so that you will feel more inclined to skip those foods you do not enjoy quite as much.
- When there is a buffet table, take only small portions of what you really want. You can always go back for more if you have not had enough.
- Try to skip dessert or else order fresh fruit without cream. Never order a soufflé or other dessert before you start a meal.

Despite all of your best intentions, you may end up in the fanciest French restaurant or in the raunchiest steak house in town. Even then, you can overcome temptation, as shown below.

In a Fancy French Restaurant:

For These	Calories	Substitute	Calories
French Onion Soup	350	Steamed mussels	120
Two rolls with butter	210	One slice French bread	70
Caesar Salad	190	Tossed salad, vinegar & oil	110
Chicken Kiev	500	Coq au vin	300
Pomme frites	200	Broccoli, lightly buttered	60
Chocolate soufflé	300	Fresh berries	80
	1750		740

In a Steak House

For These	Calories	Substitute	Calories
Sirloin, 10 ounce	1000	Filet, 6 ounce	450
French fries	285	Baked potato	100
		with margarine	100
Fried okra	230	Green beans	60
Coleslaw	140	Tossed salad with	
		vinegar and oil	80
Pecan Pie	400	Fresh fruit	80
	2055		870

As you can see, if you want to be careful, you can cut the calories, even in the most unlikely places. It only takes some attention to what you order.

REDUCE YOUR SUSCEPTIBILITY TO CANCER

Most of our concern about fat, cholesterol, and calories has been directed against the leading killer, heart disease. But cancer, #2 and coming up fast, is also very much part of the reason why we should change to the healthier diet we have advocated. The rationale is clear: as many as 35%—one out of three—cases of all cancers are related to diet.

Foods do not directly cause cancer, but they can facilitate the development of cancer, particularly those cancers arising in the intestinal tract (esophagus, stomach, colon, and rectum), genitourinary system (cervix and uterus in women, prostate in men), and breast. This list includes the most common form of cancer in women, breast, and the second most common form of cancer overall, colon. Almost certainly, changing your diet in the following ways can reduce your chances of developing cancer:

- Reduce your total fat intake.
- Eat more fiber-containing foods.
- Eat more fresh vegetables and fruits.
- Keep your weight close to the "ideal."
- Limit your alcohol intake to two or three drinks per day.
- Limit your intake of smoked, charcoal-broiled, nitrite-cured, and salt-cured foods.

Let us examine the why's and wherefore's of each of these six dietary recommendations. As we proceed, remember that cigarette smoking is a cause of another third of cancers. And do not forget the contribution of sunlight to cancers of the skin, in particular, the very malignant form, melanoma. So, by avoiding cigarettes and sunlight and by changing our diets, we have the ability to reduce our susceptibility to more than two-thirds of all cancer.

Reduce Fat Intake

We have already seen how saturated fats are involved in heart disease. Fat consumption, however, is also a likely factor in causing cancer in at least two ways: first, fats in the diet can interact with bile and bacteria in the stomach to produce cancer-producing substances; second, excess fat tissue in the body can increase the levels of estrogen, the female hormone that can stimulate the development of malignant cells in the breast and in the uterus (28). Therefore, people who eat larger amounts of fat and who are overweight have more cancers, particularly of the reproductive organs—breast in women, prostate in men—and in the colon. Obviously, you can be overweight without having eaten an excessive amount of fat, but it is quite likely that a large part of a person's extra calories comes from fat, because it is such a major component of the American diet and fat is so much richer in calories than either protein or carbohydrate.

So, if you cut out the fat in your diet in the manner described previously, not only will you look better, but also you will reduce your risk for cancer and heart disease.

More Fiber

Those people who eat more fiber will probably have less cancer of the colon and rectum as well as less trouble from inflammation of the intestines (diverticulitis and irritable bowel syndrome) and, the bane of modern man and woman, hemorrhoids. The reason for all of these effects seems to be related largely to the increased bulk of intestinal contents and the stool. Non-absorbed fiber stays in the intestinal tract absorbing water (and presumably cancer-provoking substances) and increasing the softness and size of the stool, so that there is less need to strain and cause hemorrhoids.

Fiber comes in many guises, mostly in vegetables, in fruits, and in whole grains (Table 2.8). The fiber in various foods is of multiple types, but the most important distinction is whether the fiber is capable of being fermented by bacteria in the gut, e.g. gum arabic and pectin from oats, fruits, vegetables, and legumes, or whether it is not fermentable, e.g. wheat bran and whole grains. The former fibers, which tend to be soluble, will increase gas; the latter fibers, which are insoluble, pass through the intestines almost intact and prevent constipation. Both forms have some beneficial effects, and the best policy seems to be to eat a portion of insoluble wheat bran in the form of a cereal, and to consume a couple of fiber-rich vegetables or fruits each day (29). There is a current craze for oat bran which, as a soluble fiber, may hold on to cholesterol in the gut thus preventing cholesterol from getting into the body. But peas and beans will probably do as well.

Lettuce, like conversation, requires a good deal of oil,
to avoid friction and to keep the company smooth.
—Charles Dudley Warner

Particularly with the fermentable fibers, you may need to watch out for the extra intestinal gas that may come along from the action of gut bacteria upon the fiber. If you are lucky, and if you increase your fiber intake gradually up to a maximum around thirty grams a day, you will not experience too much gas. However, as good as baked beans may be, you need only to recall the scene around the campfire in the movie, "Blazing Saddles," to remind yourself of their potential for gassy mischief.

TABLE 2.8
GOOD SOURCES OF FIBER

Food	Serving Size	Grams of Fiber
Bran cereals	1/2 cup	up to 13.5
Baked beans	1/2 cup	8.3
Apple	1 medium	4.5
Broccoli	1 medium stalk	7.4
Spinach	1/2 cup	5.7
Kidney beans	1/2 cup	4.5
Peas	1/2 cup	4.2
Banana	1 medium	4.0
Corn	1/2 cup	3.9
Potato	1 medium	3.9
Lima beans	1/2 cup	3.5
Brown rice	1/2 cup	2.8
Raisins	1/4 cup	2.5
Brussel sprouts	4	2.5
Peanut butter	2 tablespoons	2.4

More Fresh Vegetables and Fruits

In addition to their fiber, many fresh vegetables and fruits contain large amounts of vitamins A and C (Table 2.9) that appear to be protective against cancers, most particularly those cancers arising in the lung (30). Especially for smokers who are at such high risk for lung cancer, the extra intake of vitamins A and C seems to make good sense. For the rest of us, foods rich in vitamin A (also called carotene) or vitamin C are good for lots of reasons. They are low in calories and fats, high in fiber and vitamins, and they are readily available. If you eat some of these foods each day, you do not need extra amounts of A and C from vitamin pills.

TABLE 2.9
BEST SOURCES OF VITAMINS A AND C

Best Sources Of Vitamin A (Carotene)

cantaloupes
carrots
broccoli
mangoes
spinach
sweet potatoes
squash

Best Sources of Vitamin C

apple juice, vitaminized
brussel sprouts
citrus fruits and juices
green or red pepper
strawberries

Good Sources of Vitamin A (Carotene)

apricots
beet greens
nectarines
watermelons
peaches
plums
tomatoes

Good Sources of Vitamin C

cabbage
cauliflower
potato
rutabaga
tomato

Cabbage and other members of the Brassica or Cruciferous family—broccoli, Brussels sprouts, cauliflower, rutabaga, and turnips—appear also to provide special protection against cancer of the colon. So, for lots of reasons, let's hear it for broccoli: fresh or lightly steamed, with its stems peeled—it can do wonders.

Cabbage as a food has problems. It is easy to grow, a useful source of greenery for much of the year. Yet as a vegetable it has original sin, and needs improvement. It can smell foul in the pot, linger through the house with pertinacity, and ruin a meal with its wet flab. Cabbage also has a nasty history of being good for you.
— Jane Grigson

Keep Weight Close to the "Ideal"

Enough has been said already.

Limit Alcohol

Protection against cancer is one of the many reasons to keep your alcohol intake at moderate levels, no more than two or three drinks per day. However, as we shall see, that quantity may actually be good for your heart; so, we shall not recommend abstinence. There does appear to be an increased risk of breast cancer in women who drink as little as three drinks a week. On the other hand, consumption of that amount or more will reduce their risk for heart attacks which kill many more women than breast cancer does. Those women with a family history of breast cancer probably should limit themselves to no more than two drinks per week. For the rest, a drink a day seems to provide more benefit than risk.

Limit Smoked and Cured Foods

Here we are on some tricky ground. There is no doubt that smoked foods absorb some of the tars, from the incomplete combustion of the wood or from charcoal, and that these tars are similar to those in tobacco smoke that cause cancer. And there is no doubt that the nitrites and nitrates used to preserve, to cure, or to pickle foods will increase the formation of nitrosamines which are potent cancer-causing agents in the stomach.

Nevertheless, the amount of tars in smoked foods is very small, and the amount of nitrites and nitrates present naturally in foods is greater than that added to cured meats. Beets, spinach, lettuce, and cabbage are rich in nitrites or nitrates, and their use has been claimed to reduce rather than to increase the development of cancers of the intestinal tract.

So, the best advice is to watch out for salt-cured meats, such as ham and bacon, mainly because of their calories, fat, and sodium, and a little bit because of their nitrite. Smoked and charcoal grilled foods can probably be made safer by discarding the drippings, by preventing charring, by basting with marinade or sauces, or by wrapping them in foil. However, compared to the dangers of smoking cigarettes, the danger of eating smoked foods is almost inconsequential.

Taking food and drink is a great enjoyment for healthy people, and those who do not enjoy eating seldom have much capacity for enjoyment or usefulness of any act.—Charles W. Elliot

We shall have more to say about other potentially harmful food and drink toward the end of this chapter. For now, the main message is clear—eat vegetables and watch out for fat.

Do Not Go Overboard

Our concerns about food and cancer seem to be appropriate and reasonable. Yet, some individuals go further in recognizing that many foods contain small amounts of ingredients which can cause cancer when they are given to animals in much larger amounts. These carcinogens are mostly natural ingredients of plants, and they are present probably to defend against the hordes of bacteria, insects, and animals that threaten the plants (31). A substance as benign as sassafras contains a compound, safrol, that in large amounts causes cancer in rodents. Black pepper, peanut butter, celery, spinach, and many more foods contain microscopic quantities of substances that can cause cancer when they are given over prolonged periods, and in large amounts, to animals.

Should you stop eating these foods, as some people have recommended? Of course not, because the danger is so small as to be inconsequential, and so pervasive that, if carried to its extreme, we would have to live on distilled water and little else. As Dr. Bruce Ames, a leading authority on cancer, says: "Nature is not benign. . . No human diet can be entirely free of mutagens and carcinogens" (31).

Therefore, be assured that the findings from cancer research will continue to protect us from the real dangers. We can avoid those foods and other exposures that are real threats, while we continue to enjoy our sassafras soda and peanut butter sandwiches—preferably on whole-wheat bread.

STAY IN GOOD PHYSICAL CONDITION

With all of the joggers on the streets (and in all of the places to jog that we have listed in Chapter 4), you would think that we Americans are certainly in better physical condition than in previous decades. Unfortunately, the truth is that as a group we are less fit. The reasons are obvious: for, despite a fair number of upper class yuppies out jogging every morning, there are fewer children in physical education classes (which have been cut from many schools and colleges altogether); there are fewer people walking and biking to work; and there are fewer people doing physical exertion in their work. Our fingers are doing much of the walking, and machines are doing everything else that requires exertion.

As a result, America's children are fatter and are less physically fit than in previous years. The President's Council on Physical Fitness and Sports has reported these statistics (32):

- Forty percent of boys from six to twelve years cannot do more than one pullup
- One-third of the boys, from six to twelve years, and half of the girls cannot run a mile in less than ten minutes
- The proportion of overweight children in the U.S. has increased more than 50% over the last two decades

Too Much Pain for the Gain

Another part of the current problem is our natural reaction to the craze for increasingly more exercise to achieve some hoped for but never-to-be proven goals—be they nirvana or runner's high or eternal life. "No pain, no gain" was the catch phrase of the 70s. As a result, the number of marathon runners has increased from a small group of participants to many thousands. Yet, what about the millions of people who look at them and wonder why, feeling either inadequate that they are not out pounding up Heartbreak Hill with the runners, or perhaps feeling self-righteous over appearing to know better than to do so.

However, common sense is returning. Even the father of aerobics, Dr. Kenneth Cooper, has softened his stance saying: "If you run more than 15 miles a week, it's for something other than cardiovascular fitness" (33). The evidence, in fact, is showing that even more moderate exercise will provide significant protection against heart disease. Men who perform light to moderate exercise —in gardening, in making home repairs, or in walking for 45 minutes each day—have been found to be as well protected as those who averaged three times more exercise (34).

The major reservation people have about exercise is the time it takes, time that many busy people just will not set aside. The problem has been described nicely in an analysis of the longevity of 17,000 Harvard alumni. The study found that those who performed enough physical activity to burn 2,000 calories a week lived about two years longer than those who burned off less than 500 calories a week (35). It takes about five hours of steady walking or 2.5 hours of slow jogging to burn off 2,000 calories (Table 2.10). If you exercise at such a slow pace five hours a week, for fifty-two weeks a year over thirty years, the total amount of time taken up with exercise is 7,800 hours or 330 days. Therefore, it takes almost a year to perform the 2,000 calories of slow exercise a week for thirty years to add two years of life expectancy. Some people question whether or not the pain, as limited as it may be, is worth the gain. More strenuous exercise will provide the same or even more benefit and will take a lot less time.

TABLE 2.10
CALORIES BURNED PER MINUTE
OF EXERCISE

Activity	Weight 115-150 lbs.	Weight 150-195 lbs.
Aerobic dancing	6-7	8-9
Bicycling	5-6	7-8
Golf	3-4	4-5
Jogging (5 mph)	9-10	12-13
Jogging (7 mph)	10-11	13-14
Rowing machine	5-6	7-8
Swimming	5-6	7-10
Tennis (doubles)	5-7	7-8
Walking (2 mph)	2-3	3-4
Walking (4 mph)	4-5	6-7

The Benefits of Regular Exercise

There are, of course, multiple benefits to be gained from regular aerobic or isotonic exercise, in addition to the chance to live a little longer. With regular exercise, life will be more enjoyable because you will be slimmer, more able to engage in strenuous sports, and you will be less out of breath when you run to catch the plane at O'Hare. Many people say that they feel better in general when they are in shape.

To achieve true physical conditioning, defined as an increase in your body's ability to take up oxygen, requires about thirty minutes of exercise three times a week at a level of intensity to bring your heart rate up to about 70% of your maximal heart rate. You can figure out your maximal heart rate by subtracting your age from 220. Then multiply that number by 0.7 to determine your target heart rate. For a man of forty, that rate comes out 220 - 40 = 180 X 0.7 = 126. If you exercise hard enough to keep your heart rate at 126 for thirty minutes, three times a week, you will, quite likely, get all of the physical benefit you can achieve from exercise. Of course, more or longer exercise will burn off more calories. Remember, however, that exercise is a tough way to lose weight: two beers will put back all of the calories you have burned in an hour of brisk walking.

So, do it—if it feels good. But do not feel guilty or inadequate because you cannot make yourself jog every day. Our own practice is to use the air-conditioned exercise room in our apartment house, with Audrey running on the treadmill and watching T.V., and with Norman cycling on a stationary bike and reading some medical journals. We do not feel that the time is wasted. The minimal pain should be worth the gain.

But do not be a weekend warrior, who literally may kill himself by over-strenuous exercise, limited to Saturday and Sunday after five days of virtual inactivity. If you experience bothersome muscle aches and cramps, slow down a bit and build up the exercise intensity more gradually. Encounters with tennis-elbow, shin splints, and other minor exercise-related discomforts can usually be managed by short-term use of an analgesic or non-steroidal anti-inflammatory drug (NSAID). Thereby you may be able to maintain a regular exercise program by using other muscles while the inflammation is subsiding.

While you are away from home, you should be able to maintain your exercise program, if you wish. Some of the hotels listed in Chapter 4 provide workout rooms, with jogging paths or swimming pools also on their premises. The large number of facilities listed for each one of the cities throughout the U.S. and Canada shows that hotel owners have responded to the desire of many travelers to have convenient exercise facilities while they are on the road. Besides doing workouts, you can get in lots of exercise by climbing stairs, by walking the few blocks to your next appointment, and by taking a lunch-hour stroll.

AVOID UNNECESSARY STRESS

The lunch-hour stroll is not a bad way to start handling the stresses of travel. But remember that what you cannot handle at home may be even harder to handle when you are on the road. If you are a hostile Type A person who is always under a self-imposed gun of too much work in too little time, it is unlikely that you will be able to become a cool Type B person while you are traveling. Even on a vacation trip, you will probably over-schedule activities, drive around town to find a 5-star restaurant, take in a matinee and an evening performance, stay up late and wake up early, and call the office at least three times a day. If that description fits you, you may only be able to relax by spending three weeks in some secluded spot with nothing to do and without any phones. For some individuals, that form of forced relaxation may be a torture, which turns out to be more stressful than a week in New York City or San Francisco.

We should avoid, if possible, the stresses inherent in travel. However, those stresses that are part of the actual travel time, such as jet-lag, motion sickness, and airplane food, are discussed in the next chapter.

Schizophrenia beats dining alone.—Anonymous

Stress Versus Personality Type

Before you examine the reasons why you may be more stressed during your travel, and before you look at some of the ways you can reduce your level of stress, you need to consider the definitions of the terms: stress and personality type. You have probably heard of the Type A personality type, and you have certainly heard of stress. The characteristics of both personality types can lead to trouble, and the two types often feed upon each other—however different they are.

Stress has been defined as "environmental conditions that require behavioral adjustment" (36). When something happens that sets off your body's "fight or flight" responses, or makes you change your behavior, that is a stress. It is obvious that different environmental conditions are more or less stressful. In one famous study, an argument with the boss was rated half as stressful as a person's getting married, and that, in turn, was half as stressful as getting divorced (37). The greater the level of stress, the greater the likelihood that you will, subsequently, suffer physical damage, including the most serious repercussion, a heart attack.

If you are a successful professional person, you may consider your life inherently more stressful than the life of "low-achievers." Nevertheless, in truth, those of us who have become successful may be less susceptible to heart disease. Among British civil servants, the head administrators had the lowest death rate from heart disease; the second-line professionals came next, then the clerks, and finally, worst of all, the unskilled manual workers (38) (Figure 2.6). As further evidence for the relatively protected state of those who have succeeded—the overall death rate for most successful people listed in *Who's Who* is lower than the death rate for the general population (Table 2.11). Journalists appear to be an exception, perhaps because those journalists who are most highly regarded are still taking dangerous assignments rather than sitting in protected offices.

Be that as it may, whatever your level of achievement, you cannot escape stress in modern America. Perhaps, those people who have done well have already self-selected themselves as being physically and emotionally tough. Yet, even if stress does not kill you, it can certainly make you uncomfortable. Poor handling of the extra stresses that you encounter during your travel can spoil a business deal or a vacation.

You shall have joy or you shall have power, said God.
You shall not have both.— Ralph Waldo Emerson

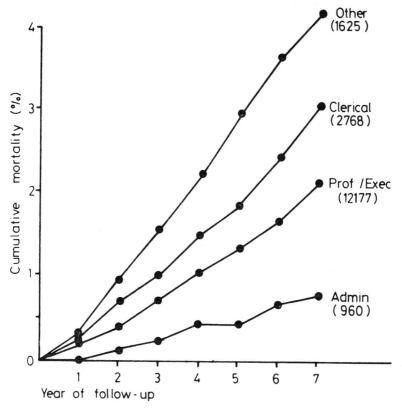

FIGURE 2.6: The cumulative mortality from coronary heart disease over 7 years among 17,530 London civil servants aged 40 to 64, classified by their employment grade. (From Rose G and Marmot MG: Br Heart J 1981;45:13).

TABLE 2.11
COMPARATIVE MORTALITY OF PROMINENT
MEN LISTED IN *WHO'S WHO**

Vocational Groups	Mortality Rate Relative to General Population (100%)
All groups	70%
Scientists	55%
College professors	61%
Clergymen	62%
Business executives	71%
Physicians	78%
Government officials	81%
Journalists	134%

*From Statistical Bulletin (January-March 1979):8.

Distinct from stress and your ability to cope with it, you also have a certain personality type. As first described by Drs. Friedman and Rosenman in San Francisco in 1955, you can be characterized as being, more or less, Type A or Type B. The easiest definition of the Type A behavioral pattern is: a syndrome characterized by a continuously harrying sense of time urgency and an easily aroused free-floating hostility (39). The critical terms are sense of time urgency and hostility. Notice, in particular, the inclusion of the term, hostility. Just because you are constantly busy, ambitious, and energetic, you are not in trouble—unless you are hostile about your life situation.

Probably, you already know if you are a Type A, but here are the major characteristics:

- Hard-driving and competitive about everything, aggressive about getting what you want.
- Doing things quickly, including eating and talking; finishing the sentences for slow-speaking people.
- Doing more than one thing at a time: opening the mail while you are talking on the phone (and even reading some of it while you are listening); thinking of other things when people talk to you.

- Easily irritated by delays, by standing in line, by interruptions.
- Losing temper easily and usually showing it.

The more of these characteristics that you have, the more "Type A" you are, and according to most, but not all, long-time studies, the more likely you are to have a heart attack. Type B's, who are easygoing, calm, relaxed, slow, patient, reflective, and unexcitable, have fewer heart attacks, and presumably they live longer. Some individuals may think that Type B's are rather boring and bored people, but maybe Type B's are just laid-back and satisfied. Nevertheless, a large number of urban American men are Type A, and more of these men are found in occupations with higher prestige and among people with higher levels of education. Because most of our knowledge about personality types has come from studies on middle-class white men, we do not know as much about other groups of people.

It is logical to assume that Type A's put themselves under more stress and that they react more violently to this stress. It is quite likely that they are in a vicious circle. Because Type A's are more stressed, they are given to more Type A behavior. The result may describe your boss and his behavior, but probably many of us are Type A's.

Nothing is so vulgar as to be in a hurry.—Oliver Wendell Holmes

Switching Your Type

Assuming that you are a Type A—and most of the successful people we know are—you might want to change your behavior, and that may be possible. You could start by reading *Treating Type A Behavior* by Dr. Friedman and Diane Ulmer (Fawcett Crest, New York, 1984). Some of the strategies specifically applicable to travel are the following:

- Simplify your life.
- Schedule fewer appointments and provide some built-in thinking/relaxing time.
- Escape from your work during lunch, even if you eat with business associates.
- Get rid of some of your tension by stretching and by progressive muscle relaxation, simple to do wherever you are.
- Take time for exercise every day.
- Read something unrelated to your work while you are on the airplane.

- Schedule a visit to a museum or engage in other nonbusiness activity during the trip.
- Call home when you are not expected to do so, just for a pleasant interlude.
- Avoid unnecessary stresses. In this age, that stress might include sex with a stranger. For some people this is a temptation while they are away from home. However, it is more of a danger these days than ever before.

The Extra Stresses of Travel

In addition to trying to change your underlying personality, you should consider now some extra stresses which are posed by travel and which need to be addressed. We have already discussed most of these stresses briefly in Chapter 1, but we need to look at a few more.

To begin, you must consider the purpose of your trip. Is the trip for business or pleasure? Some individuals keep the two apart, but many, at least on travel to popular places, combine the two. That seems to be a good idea, but you should recognize some of the potential stresses:

- Your business commitments may develop beyond what you had anticipated, thereby cutting into the time you are able to spend with your spouse, possibly provoking some resentment in him or her.
- You may be so tired from a long day of work that when you go out for a big night on the town, you end up falling asleep in the soup, or, perhaps, not even waiting for the first act of the play. You may not realize what your work has taken out of you physically and emotionally. There may not be enough time left over in your schedule for fun and games.

No man is lonely while eating spaghetti. — Robert Morley

- The places you visit on business may not be the places you would really like to spend time in for pleasure. (It may take a few more dollars for you to go on a trip purely for pleasure, but the cost may well be worth it.) Going away where you will be without the necessity of speeches, sales pitches, or appointments to make, may permit you to get the ultimate pleasure and relaxation from your vacation.

Besides the potential problems of mixing a business trip with a pleasure trip, travel may be stressful because of the breaks from your home routine, because of the added physical demands of travel, and because of the extra expectations of what you hope to accomplish. We seldom run out of work on the road, and most of us return home with only part of what we have taken to do being completed.

A last word about the stresses of travel. You should recognize that you are particularly susceptible to having a heart attack at certain times, which just may be the times you have taken on more travel. Perhaps after a divorce or after the death of a spouse or after taking on a new job, you may feel the need for additional travel. Be careful, however, because these circumstances and other significant life events may set you up, and the travel may finish you off.

Managing the Stresses of Travel

Travel, like life, will never be stress-free. No stress means no life, and a little stress keeps the juices flowing. But we need to remove the stresses that are unnecessary and to reduce the level of those that we cannot avoid.

The steps for avoiding unnecessary stress are both simple and complex: insisting on a quiet hotel room away from the noise of the street, all the way to your spending a few hours of pure leisure in the middle of a hectic schedule. One of the most obvious ways to avoid stress is to eat and to drink moderately, and then to get enough sleep the night before a day filled with important appointments. Perhaps you can recall the nights you had too much food and much too much booze, followed by hours of fitful and inadequate sleep before you got up to give a major address or before you attended a critical negotiating session.

Some Techniques to Reduce the Stresses of Travel

We have mentioned some tricks we have learned to enable you to sleep better and to avoid jet-lag or motion sickness, along with some of the other physical stresses of travel. Here are additional ways of reducing stresses, especially emotional stresses:

- Always reserve your airplane seat ahead of time, and when possible, have a boarding pass delivered to you with the ticket.
- Join and use the airline's airport club which is most suited to your travel needs.

You will also find more and better equipped and staffed Business Service Centers at the major airports, facilities which provide photocopy and secretarial service, facsimile transmission and reception, express mail, etc. Before long, you will be going to the airport two hours early to get your work done.

- If you anticipate arriving at your destination near or after 6:00 p.m., you should guarantee your hotel room with a credit card.
- Use a luggage caddy, or even better, get a Sky Valet (Athalon Products, 3333 E. 52nd Avenue, Denver, CO 80216) which has rollers and a rigid (but collapsible) support for the easiest-to-use carry-on luggage we have ever seen.
- Carry your luggage on board. As of January 1, 1988, the FAA has limited the size and number of carry-on luggage, the regulations accommodating the spaces available on the particular type of airplane you fly. Similar to the Sky Valet in most ways, except for the rollers, a System Four Valet bag marketed by Samsonite combines a suitcase and a garment bag in one easy-to-carry piece that will fit under most airline seats or in an overhead compartment. Take less and pack tightly, so that you can carry it on board and stow it safely.
- Use some of the rapidly expanding supply of portable work enhancers that can be carried onboard—including computers and word processors, facsimile machines, photocopiers, and even battery-operated VCR's.

If this technology keeps developing, you will not need to stay in your office or at the airport to get your work done; you can do it all onboard your flight. However, all of these machines make us nervous, and we rather like the idea of having to read a book or some magazines en route. Ah, well, we do not like to see the air phones either, and we have continued to resist putting in car phones. We are not the busy executive types—always having to make deals and always having to stay in touch with someone. We have often wondered if a few of those calls are not to some bookie. But whatever turns you on is okay. Just remember, however, that your psyche and your heart may need to be turned off, on occasion.

The Benefits of Doing Nothing

The last step in avoiding stress may be the hardest. Recognize and accept the lasting value of doing absolutely nothing on occasion. Most of us behave now like Alice in Wonderland, in running faster and faster just to stay even. Our current situation has been described by Jeremy Rifkin in *Time Wars: The Primary Conflict in Human History* (Henry Holt: New York, 1987):

> Every society has its unique tempo, and nothing so captures the American tempo as the word "speed." We are a nation in love with speed. We drive fast, eat fast, make love fast. We digest our life, condense our experiences, and compress our thoughts. While other cultures might believe that haste makes waste, we are convinced that speed reflects alertness, power, and success.

The solution to our society's ever-increasing demand for speed and expansion is described well by Bertrand Russell, one of the greatest intellects of all time, when he advocates in all seriousness a four-hour work day. Reflecting in an essay from *In Praise of Idleness and Other Essays* (Unwin and Hyman: London, 1935), Russell writes:

> I think that there is far too much work done in the world, that immense harm is caused by the belief that work is virtuous, and that what needs to be preached in modern industrial countries is quite different from what always has been preached. . . .

> . . .leisure is essential to civilization, and in former times leisure for the few was only rendered possible by the labors of the many. Their labors were valuable, not because work is good, but because leisure is good. And with modern labor-saving techniques it would be possible to distribute leisure justly without injury to civilization.

> . . .if the ordinary wage earner worked four hours a day, there would be enough for everybody, and no unemployment - assuming a certain very moderate amount of sensible organization. This idea shocks the well-to-do, because they are convinced that the poor would not know how to use so much leisure. In America, men often work long hours even when they are already well off; such men, naturally, are indignant at the idea of leisure for wage earners, except as the grim punishment of unemployment.

The wise use of leisure, it must be conceded, is a product of civilization and education. A man who has worked long hours all his life will be bored if he becomes suddenly idle. But without a considerable amount of leisure a man is cut off from many of the best things. There is no longer any reason why the bulk of the population should suffer this deprivation; only a foolish asceticism makes us continue to insist on work in excessive quantities now that the need no longer exists.

Russell's reflections, fifty years later, may seem to be the impossible dream of an undisciplined philosopher. However, there is truth in what he says, and we would all be better off if we were to take his advice.

Because everyone else seems to be addicted to even more work, the best relief you can have may be to spend at least some free time during your travels, really doing nothing. For some people that plan may turn out to be counterproductive. If so, instead you may need to take a quiet walk, perhaps a stroll through an art museum, or would you believe it, you may need to go back to your hotel for a nap. That practice, embodied in the after-lunch siesta may, in fact, have scientific justification. Recent studies show that the human body is strongly programmed for a midday nap (40). However, the body has been overwhelmed by work schedules and by the caffeine in coffee and Cokes. If only there were a couch in the office and if only there were no phones. Yet, even if these conditions prevailed, you would probably feel guilty napping while the rest of the world was computing.

KEEP TOXIC SUBSTANCES OUT OF YOUR BODY

The last of our steps toward better health may indeed be the most difficult because we may have little control of what we breathe, eat or drink.

That caffeine we use to overcome our natural body programming may be one of the substances we need to avoid. In truth, moderate amounts of caffeine do not seem to be in any way harmful for most of us, but there are some people who cannot sleep at night because they actually have withdrawal symptoms from the caffeine contained in twelve or more cups of strong coffee a day. For those individuals, moderation is needed (as it is for most things).

Some substances are so toxic they should be completely avoided: cocaine comes quickest to mind. Other substances may be tolerated without obvious trouble as long as they are kept within bounds. Alcohol, caffeine and some would argue marijuana, are examples. Yet, other substances, often blamed for various ills, probably do not deserve the bad reputation—for example, sugar, saccharin, and aspartame. Lastly, there is evidence that protein, one of the three major types of food, may fit into the middle category; for while moderate amounts of protein are good, in the excessive amounts we are now consuming, harm may occur.

Most likely, we have said enough about coffee. If you are drinking fewer than six cups a day, you may not suffer any ill effects. However, we have noticed that as we have grown older, we are unable to drink coffee past about 8:00 p.m., if we want to fall asleep by midnight. Even so, we would hate to face the next day without at least one, and preferably two cups of coffee in the morning.

Sex on the Road and AIDS

Another "toxin" to which travelers may be exposed is the AIDS virus. Whether married or not, many individuals give in to the temptations of sex on the road—for various reasons: more contacts with attractive people, many of whom share similar professional interests; more drinking of alcohol which may lower their levels of both good sense and sexual inhibition; and more "empty" time in the secret spaces of out-of-town hotels.

AIDS is the latest, and certainly the worst of sexually transmitted diseases. By comparison, herpes and gonorrhea seem innocuous. Indeed, as we are becoming increasingly aware of the possibility of transmitting the AIDS virus by heterosexual or "ordinary" sex, it is obvious that sex with a stranger—or even with someone you know quite well, but only see occasionally—is a major risk of travel. To show what can happen, consider that a 40-year-old heterosexual man developed AIDS after only two sexual contacts with the same infected carrier three years previously (41).

Single's bars are certainly not as busy as they used to be, and one-night stands seem to be on their way out. Because even the supposedly safe practice of straight sex—using a condom—may not be totally safe, more and more people are being celibate when they are away from a spouse or usual sex partner. Remember that when condoms are carefully used for contraception, there is a failure (pregnancy) rate of at least two per 100, and maybe as high as ten per 100.

73

The AIDS virus is a million times smaller than sperm; so, if sperm can get through the condom that often, just think about the potential for a virus.

The only safe sex is with a safe partner, one who has never been infected with the AIDS virus. Sex with such a partner is safe regardless of how it is done, orally, rectally, or vaginally. However, if your partner is not safe, sex by any route may be lethal.

Can you be sure your partner is safe? Certainly, if your partner is your spouse or long-time mate, whom you trust and know. Certainly not, if your partner is a pick-up, or much worse, a prostitute. Perhaps if an instant AIDS test becomes available—a highly unlikely possibility—you could feel safer in going to bed with a new partner. Remember, however, that no test is apt to tell if your partner has been infected recently and is already capable of passing it on. So, have fun—and practice all of the non-intercourse techniques that may give you sexual gratification. But, follow your mother's advice, and do not mess around, unless you are involved in a long-time relationship with someone whom you trust. We doubt that such trust can ever be based upon the contacts made during short-time travel, particularly when the contact occurs after a few drinks, and especially because the most popular cities we travel to are often those cities with the highest rate of AIDS. Abstinence on the road is the best policy. However, you might take along your long-time mate for the fun.

Sexual pursuit burns calories to boot.—Audrey Kaplan

If, despite the warnings, you still seek sex with a new partner, especially when you do not have the luxury of checking a blood test or of waiting six months to see if the person has a latent infection, there are ways to minimize your risk:

- Choose a partner who has had the fewest number of other partners.
- Choose a partner who has only engaged in heterosexual sex, using condoms, not involving anal penetration.
- Choose a partner who has not used I.V. drugs or has not had a transfusion in the past five years.
- Choose a partner who lives in South or North Dakota, where only eight cases of AIDS have been reported since the disease was first recognized in 1981.
- Perform sex with a well-fitted condom that has been pre-tested for leaks.

Some people have suggested that those who wish to engage in sex with a new partner should both provide his or her own negative AIDS test and should require one from the partner. That procedure hardly seems practical, even if AIDS testing becomes much more widespread. Remember that current (and probably future) AIDS testing does not rule out the possibility of a person's recent infection, before the six months it takes the body to develop the antibodies that are measured in the test but when spread of the virus is possible.

Lastly, we decry the hysteria about non-intimate, non-sexual contacts with AIDS victims or with those who have positive AIDS tests. Such people, obviously, must not expose unknowing individuals to risk, but we should not ostracize or avoid ordinary contacts with them. There is no evidence that breathing the same air, or that touching them, or having other casual contacts with them will spread the virus.

Alcohol

In moderate amounts, one to three drinks a day, alcohol (ethanol) should not cause either acute intoxication or chronic damage to any part of the body. Such amounts, in fact, appear to reduce the development of heart disease. Larger amounts cause all kinds of trouble, from drunk driving and liver damage to more cancer, in addition to the tremendous social disruptions of alcohol addiction. Two disclaimers: the fetus may be damaged by fairly small amounts; so, pregnancy seems to be a time for abstinence (as with most drugs and foreign substances); and two epidemiological surveys have reported a higher rate of breast cancer among women who drank more than three drinks a week (42, 43), considerably less than we have advised. That evidence needs to be confirmed, but until it is, women whose mothers have had breast cancer, or women who are more susceptible because of their obesity or their high saturated fat diet may be wise in keeping their consumption below what we have recommended.

For most people, home and away, drinking one to three bottles of beer or glasses of wine or shots of whiskey a day should help you to relax, to release a few of your inhibitions, to compliment the taste of your entrée—and should help to protect your coronaries at the same time. As you can see (Table 2.12), the amount of alcohol in one usual drink—twelve ounces of beer, four ounces of wine, one-and-a-half ounces of distilled spirits—gives you about fifteen millimeters or one-half ounce of alcohol.

TABLE 2.12
THE ALCOHOL CONTENT OF VARIOUS DRINKS

Distilled spirits (whiskey, vodka, rum, gin)
80 proof = 40% alcohol
1½ ounces = 18 milliliters of alcohol

Wine = 12% alcohol
4 ounces = 14.4 milliliters of alcohol

Beer = 4.5% alcohol
12 ounces = 16.2 milliliters of alcohol

Although some people claim the special advantages of one form of booze over another, the forms are probably all alike. Most forms of alcohol also provide the same number of calories, about 100 in each drink (But watch out for the mixes which will add another 100 or so). Now, it is true that if you gulp down three martinis on an empty stomach, you will certainly raise your blood alcohol level more rapidly, and to a higher level, than if you sip three glasses of wine during a two-hour dinner. Your body can easily metabolize the alcohol in about one drink each hour, so you should not have any trouble at that level. It is also true that people vary in how they handle alcohol and in how it affects them. So, if you know you get soused with only two glasses of wine, you should keep yourself below that level, if your purpose is to socialize and not to get bombed.

One of the disadvantages of wine is that it makes a
man mistake words for thoughts. — Samuel Johnson

How does alcohol reduce your chances of having a heart attack? We are still not sure, although there has been a steady increase in the number of studies that have shown a lower rate of heart attacks in those who drink one to three drinks a day. Most studies show what was found among British civil servants (Figure 2.7), who had a significantly lower death rate from all causes (total) and from cardiovascular disease (CVD) if they had consumed nine to thirty-four grams of alcohol a day, the equivalent of one to three drinks. Those people who had drunk more still had a lower death rate from heart diseases, but they had more deaths from non-cardiovascular diseases, including such things as trauma, cancer, and liver disease.

The protective effect of one to three drinks a day may arise from the effect of alcohol in raising the levels of the good form of cholesterol, the HDL fraction which, as we have noted, provides protection by helping to remove the bad form (LDL cholesterol) from the blood vessels. A little alcohol may also lower the blood pressure, and it may reduce the impact of psychological stress.

Those individuals who choose not to drink for religious or other reasons should not feel endangered. The protection provided by alcohol can be achieved through exercise and weight control; and, most likely, such people do not smoke or engage in other potentially harmful life styles.

Our approach should not be taken as a defense of alcohol abuse: the social and physical damages of heavy alcohol consumption have led many people to preach a return to prohibition. We think that the advocacy of small amounts of regular alcohol consumption is medically sound advice for most individuals. The apparent benefits can be obtained from one portion a day. Therefore, a glass of wine with dinner will give you all the good and none of the bad effects.

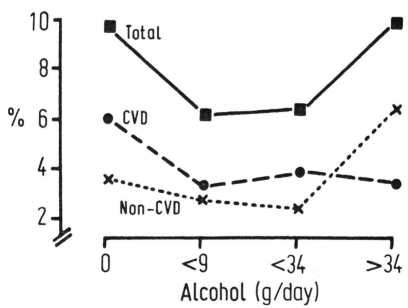

FIGURE 2.7: The percentage rates of death from all causes (total), cardiovascular diseases (CVD), and noncardiovascular (non-CVD) causes according to daily average alcohol consumption in 10 years among 1,422 civil servants in London. (From Marmot MG, et al: Lancet 1981;1:578). (One gram [g] is approximately equal to one milliliter.)

77

Sugar

Pure sugar is blamed for cavities (probably true), heart disease (not true), cancer (not true), and for simply being "empty calories"— that is, without vitamins, minerals, or other assorted goodies. If you are eating a reasonably balanced meal, you do not need all the other goodies from sugar; so, we see no reason to cut out all of the natural sweets and the use of sugar in moderate amounts. A three-year study of over 1,000 reports has concluded that moderate sugar consumption is not a risk (44).

There seems to be little reason to substitute saccharin or aspartamate for the seventeen calories you get in a teaspoonful of sugar. However, if you drink so much coffee and so many Cokes that the teaspoonfuls would add up to a lot of calories, or if you just feel more righteous if you use the substitutes instead of sugar, there seems to be no reason not to do so. Concerns about their safety appear to be unfounded.

Protein

Unlike sugar, protein continues to get good press, with many beef, pork, chicken, and cheese providers extolling the virtues of high protein intake. In truth, our average consumption of protein is far in excess of our body's needs and our body's ability to handle protein (45). We have to excrete therefore a larger amount of the waste products of protein (urea, creatinine, uric acid) through the kidneys than they are capable of handling easily, and there is a growing amount of evidence that various kidney problems are caused or are aggravated by our typically high protein diet. And remember that red meat, the major source of protein, also contains lots of that old demon—saturated fat.

The best advice is to cut down your protein intake to about fifteen percent of your total calories. For those taking 2,000 calories a day, that would be 300 calories or about seventy-five grams (2 1/2 ounces) of protein or what is in a smallish portion of chicken, cheese, or meat; so, one portion a day should give you all you need. You can get the necessary protein for the essential amino acids from vegetables alone. So, meat consumption really is not necessary.

Because muscle is largely made up of protein, some body-builders, athletes, and perhaps week-end jocks may have been brainwashed into believing that they need extra protein. Your body can make muscle from other sources, and there is really no need for twelve-ounce steaks and lots of protein supplements as provided on the training tables for many athletic teams. They are only raising their cholesterol levels (from the saturated fat), and they are stressing their kidneys unnecessarily.

Vitamins and Mineral Supplements

Here again, you probably do not need any more than what a well-balanced diet provides (46). Too much of the fat soluble vitamins, A and D, which are stored in the body, may be harmful. Large amounts of the water soluble vitamins, such as B and C, do not seem to hurt. And some people assume that they can stop a cold with extra vitamin C, a claim we do not think has been documented.

Food Preservatives and Additives

There have been some legitimate concerns about nitrites, as noted before, and about hormones and food dyes and a variety of other foreign substances added to foods to preserve them or to enhance their appeal. Large amounts of them, such as monosodium glutamate (MSG) used in Chinese and other foods, may cause such symptoms as weakness and headaches. Those people who are concerned enough to return to an all-natural diet may have good reason to do so, but we are convinced that the processors of food and the Food and Drug Administration really protect us very well, while they provide us with the kinds of food we want.

That is not to say they could not and should not do better. We are not worried about the preservatives and additives; it is the "food porn" with too much fat, too much protein, too many calories that all of us, and particularly our children, are being enticed to eat. Credit must be given to the people at the Center for Science in the Public Interest who, through their monthly magazine, *Nutrition Action,* and through their adversary role protect us from most of the excesses. We agree with almost all of their positions, although every so often they seem to go off on possibly excessive tangents. If you are interested in promoting better nutrition, as all of us should, consider contributing to CSPI and reading *Nutrition Action.*

And Let's Hear It for Aspirin

As you can tell, our general posture is to avoid all foreign substances, if possible. That should apply to most drugs, unless you need them. However, one drug, in particular, seems to be useful for a lot of us, the old standby—aspirin. The evidence is not in completely, but so far there is considerable support for aspirin's protective action against heart attacks and strokes, through very small amounts of the acetyl part of acetylsalicylic acid (better known as aspirin).

The protection involves the inactivation, by the acetyl part of aspirin, of certain enzymes which are needed to make some hormones, called thromboxanes, which cause blood vessels to constrict and blood clots to form. These hormones are needed when you cut yourself, to limit the loss of blood. However, they also appear to be involved in the clotting of blood that occurs where there is roughening of the lining of blood vessels, a process which in turn may block off the blood supply to the heart (leading to a heart attack) or to the brain (leading to a stroke).

Fortunately, it takes only a touch of aspirin to do the job. One-quarter of a regular tablet, the amount in a child's aspirin, taken every two days will, most likely, provide all of the needed protection with fewer of the possible side effects of larger amounts. So, on the road or at home, a little aspirin, as in a child's portion (81 mg) every other day, should really help to keep the doctor away.

The Final Words

Our advice, intended to keep the traveler healthy, should enhance his or her enjoyment of the trip. Our dietary guidelines fit very closely with those of the expert committee of the American Heart Association (47) (Table 2.13) as well as those guidelines in the 1988 Surgeon General's Report on Nutrition and Health.

In addition to our urging a healthy diet, we have also advised in favor of some practices or advised against some others.

Finally, we can proclaim no better advice than that which is attributed to Satchel Paige who, during his time, was one of baseball's greatest pitchers (but whose best time preceded Jackie Robinson's breaking the color barrier of big league sports).

Satch suggested six rules for a happy life:

- Avoid fried meats which angry up the blood.
- If your stomach disputes you, lie down and pacify it with cool thoughts.
- Keep the juices flowing by jangling around gently as you move.
- Go very lightly on vices such as carrying on in society; the social ramble ain't restful.
- Avoid running at all times.
- Don't look back. Someone may be gaining on you.

TABLE 2.13
DIETARY GUIDELINES FOR HEALTHY AMERICAN ADULTS
(Nutrition Committee, American Heart Association Circulation 1986;74:1465A)

1. Saturated fat intake should be less than 10% of calories.
2. Total fat intake should be less than 30% of calories.
3. Cholesterol intake should be less than 100 mg/1,000 cal, not to exceed 300 mg/day.
4. Protein intake should be approximately 15% of calories.
5. Carbohydrate intake should constitute 50 to 55% or more of calories, with emphasis on increased complex carbohydrates.
6. Sodium intake should be reduced to approximately 1 g/1,000 cal, not to exceed 3 g/day.
7. If alcoholic beverages are consumed, the caloric intake from this source should be limited to 15% of total calories but should not exceed 50 ml. of ethanol per day.
8. Total calories should be sufficient to maintain the individual's best body weight.*
9. A wide variety of foods should be consumed.

*Metropolitan Tables of Height and Weight, Table of Desirable Weights for Men and Women. Metropolitan Life Insurance Company, 1959.

Chapter 3
Staying Alive At 35,000 Feet

*I always love to begin a journey on Sundays, because I
shall have the prayers of the church to preserve all that
travel by land, or by water.—*
Jonathan Swift, 1667-1745

Sunday, or even better, the Jewish Sabbath, Saturday, is still a better day to travel because there are fewer flyers on weekends than on most week days. However, the reasons for Swift's preferring to start his travel on a Sunday 250 years ago hardly apply to today's travel which usually starts and finishes within hours.

Obviously, travel today is faster, safer and more comfortable. Yet, even under the best circumstances, travel can still be stressful. And that does not necessarily include the taxi ride from La Guardia into mid-Manhattan, which these days can be a death-defying act with a driver who does not speak English, who does not know where Fifth Avenue is, and who drives his non-shock absorbing tank over the potholes of New York City either at sixty miles per hour between red lights or at two miles an hour across town. (Where have the old cabbies gone?)

New York taxis may be one problem, but there are many more problems in just reaching your destination. Most of what follows relates to air travel because that is what well over one million of us do every day.

Relax and Try to Enjoy

Before we delve into the problems further, let us consider the overall attitude that most American business people seem to bring with them on the airplane—that of "business as usual." Men dressed in their three piece dark suits, or women in their high collars and proper skirts below the knees, seem mostly to be on their way to the office. However, consider that, unless you must take a cab directly from the airport to an appointment, there seems to be little sense in your being all spruced up on the airplane. If you are planning to check in at the hotel first, you can always travel comfortably and still get to your appointment after a quick change.

Air travel calls for light, loose clothing, comfortable shoes, and a relaxed attitude. Consequently, we can get some of our best reading done, and if necessary, we can work while we are at 35,000 feet, away from the phone and other interruptions. All we need is a window seat and no two-year-old rowdies in the next one.

Overcoming the Fear of Flying

A few people have a serious phobia about heights in general and flying in particular. Many more of us have serious concerns about the safety of air travel in the U.S. these days, and almost all of us are bothered by the delays and the inconveniences that seem to be getting progressively worse.

With regard to the real acrophobics, psychologists apparently can help most people overcome their unfounded fears. This usually requires a series of three or more structured sessions, with the last involving an actual flight. After such therapy, most acrophobics can successfully take flights on their own (48).

For those of us concerned about safety, we need to consider the facts: travel on U.S. commercial airlines is the safest form of transportation ever known. In 1986, only half as many deaths occurred per flying hour than in 1978, and flying still remains a great deal safer, per mile of travel, than do driving or walking. The problem, obviously, is that the crash of one plane, carrying 200 passengers, every six months or so, commands a great deal more attention than the hundreds of daily car collisions that each day kill an average of 126 people in the U.S. alone. Air crashes make a hell of a louder noise than almost any other tragedies do, save the sinking of a major passenger ship or a train wreck, when similarly large numbers of people are killed.

Flying seems to be more dangerous than driving for another reason: you have no control over what happens, and you have a growing distrust of the competency of the system. Despite the facts concerning the safety of commercial airlines, we have a fear of mid-air collisions. Our fears are heightened by the realization that twice as many people are flying today than ten years ago and by the perception that maintenance and operations simply are not keeping up with the demands. Every time there is a delay, the thought must arise that things are going wrong and that there is danger lurking in the friendly skies.

The U.S. government and U.S. airlines are trying harder to resolve the problems of delays and near-collisions. Flights are being rescheduled, and the numbers of delays are being disclosed. However, critics have pointed out an underlying need for the additional spending of some of the $5.6 billion surplus that lies unused in the Aviation Trust Fund, accumulated from an eight percent excise tax on airline tickets. With additional personnel and with advanced technology and more airport runway space, flying can be made even safer than it already is. As a traveler, you have the responsibility to speak up—to your congressman, to the FAA, and to the airlines—about the need for further changes.

These global problems are not the only ones you face. Most other problems are more mundane, such as in-flight meals, lost luggage, and jet-lag.

Eating In-Flight

It is really rather remarkable that so many people can be fed as efficiently as they are during air travel. The food is delivered reasonably hot and served within a very short interval to a lot of people. Compare what 350 people get on a DC-10 to what the same number of people receive at most banquets at the largest hotel in town. (If only they could heat up the rolls!)

That is not to say the food served on airplanes is nature's best. Witness our recent meal on one of the major carriers: mixed green salad (+) with rich, creamy dressing (-); a four-ounce steak (-); overcooked green beans (+); half a potato mashed and glopped back into the skin (+); cheesecake (-); roll and butter (-). As you can see, the minuses outweigh the pluses. All of these servings came without choices, unlike what American Airlines and other airlines often do in providing a meat or a chicken entrée, or a pasta, and a fish salad. We were particularly encouraged with the regular dinner on a recent American Airlines flight that included low salt peanuts, polyunsaturated margarine, Italian dressing for the salad, chicken with rice and greens, and three pieces of chocolate for dessert—all together a most healthy diet.

In truth, better choices are available, if you ask for them ahead of time, usually six hours before your departure, but preferably when you make your reservations. Every major airline serves a variety of meals when you make a special request (Table 3.1). If you are really interested in maintaining your low-calorie and low-cholesterol or low-sodium diet, you can do it by a little pre-planning. These special meals are available on Coach. In First Class you are usually offered enough choices that you can pick and choose what you want.

When all is said and done, it really seems silly for us to expect gourmet food at 35,000 feet. Yes, it can be done—we have had the wonderful experience of flying First Class to Europe. The excellent dinner on that flight cost well over $40, considerably beyond the $4 or $5 spent on most domestic Coach dinners. However, it seems to be a lot more sensible to expect a nice green salad, cold pasta, or a pita sandwich along with some fresh fruit for dessert, rather than a heavy meal with all the trimmings.

TABLE 3.1
AIRLINE MENU OPTIONS

Airline	Bland	Diabetic	Vegetarian	Fruit	Seafood	Kosher	Low Calorie/Cholesterol	Low Sodium
American	+	+	+	+	+	+	+	+
Braniff	-	-	-	+	-	+	-	-
Continental	-	+	+	+	-	+	-	-
Delta	+	+	+	+	+	+	+	+
Eastern	+	+	+	+	+	+	+	-
Northwest	+	-	+	+	-	+	+	+
Pan American	+	+	+	+	+	+	+	+
Piedmont	+	+	+	+	+	+	+	+
TWA	-	+	+	-	-	+	+	+
United	+	+	+	-	-	+	+	+
U.S. Air	-	+	+	-	-	+	+	+

86

Some people find that of all the special meals, Kosher comes out best. For us, that depends on whether it is prepared fresh or stored frozen in the airline commissary and thawed during the flight. Frankly, the problem with Kosher meals describes the overall problem of airline food: the airlines depend upon caterers who must prepare literally thousands of similar meals each day and get them to the right flight. Most times, reasonably tasty, hygenic meals with hot entrées and cold drinks are available. However, for us, in-flight food service seems to be among the least important problems most travelers face.

Drinking and Flying

The dry air in the cabin and your natural tendency to breathe a little heavier will cause you to dehydrate a bit during long flights. You should drink lots of fluids, probably a glassful every hour or so. Those fluids logically may include one or two alcohol-containing drinks, but do not drink alcohol-containing beverages as your only source of fluids en route. Because alcohol may increase your urine flow, you may end up lacking in your total body fluid content. It is better to take no more than one or two alcohol-containing drinks and at least an equal number of drinks without alcohol.

In addition to alcohol's diuretic action, there are other reasons not to drink as much alcohol as many people do during their air travel. It seems that drinks poured from those little bottles do not register with people as containing as much alcohol as from the larger bottles. Or, more likely, with the anxiety and the boredom of long flights, even people who are usually teetotalers tend to drink. Not that three or four drinks during a five-hour transcontinental flight will necessarily do you in, but do not blame your inability to sleep that night or your hangover and poor performance the next day on jet-lag.

Airline personnel do have a responsibility to curtail the excessive amount of alcohol drinking in which some passengers indulge. We have encountered some awfully obnoxious drunks during our long flights, and those people would not get that way unless they were being provided with the alcohol. It is obviously more of a problem in First Class when you are repeatedly offered free drinks. As we have observed before, moderation is the best practice, but sometimes the temptations do make it easy for people to stray.

Staying Fit on Board

If you stay in your seat during a flight that is over two hours, you have been sitting too long. Airplanes are not made for jogging, but you should get up and walk around, stretching a bit every hour or so. That may be a problem during long food service, but dodging carts can be an exercise in itself. While you are seated, you can do various exercises, from stamping your feet to hunching your shoulders, exercises that will not disturb the passenger in the next seat. Do a progressive tightening and loosening of every group of muscles, or move every joint in your body. The idea is more to keep the blood circulating than to burn off calories. Prolonged motionless seating, with the legs down and the venous drainage constricted by the edge of the seat, can slow the circulation enough in the legs to cause blood clots to form in people already at risk. Most of us, however, are not that susceptible, but a bit of movement certainly will not hurt.

On really long flights, it is more important to get up and walk around the plane. Your muscles will not become stiff and sore, and you will not feel as tired when you arrive. Moreover, movement will tend to reduce the swelling of your feet and ankles that commonly occurs—partly because of keeping your feet down and partly because of gravitational pull.

Sleep may be a problem, particularly on full flights with seats that barely recline. We have found it much easier to sleep with a combination of sponge ear plugs (available in some airline kits provided on overseas flights or at airports for about $1.00), with eye shades, and with a little blow-up pillow called a Headbed (available at airport shops) which keeps your head from plopping down on your chest or shoulders, eventually giving you a really stiff neck. We always ask for window seats that usually provide more head support. And, of course, it is bliss when we have a row of empty seats with removable arm rests so that we can really stretch out.

If you still have trouble, a short-acting sedative may do wonders. It is important to remember that even so-called "mild" sedatives may be habit-forming and should be taken only under a physician's advice. Over-the-counter sleep-aids are often either too weak or too long-acting to be of much help. Be aware, moreover, that alcohol does not lead to relaxed sleep. You may doze, but you will not wake up refreshed. It is a lot safer and more efficient to take a short-acting sedative than a load of booze to get some good sleep on board.

Handling Jet-Lag

If you travel quickly over three time zones, most likely you will experience jet-lag after you arrive (49). You may have trouble sleeping, a feeling of general discomfort, a disruption of appetite and bowel habits, reduced psychological and physical alertness and efficiency. If it is really severe, as after a sixteen-hour flight from Japan, you may experience, as one of us did, spatial disorientation to the degree that the right leg pushed on the accelerator when the intent was for the left leg to push on the clutch. The car ended up almost a total wreck, and so did the other one of us who was not wearing a seatbelt at the time.

Fortunately, the only trouble that most people have with jet-lag is not sleeping through the night. But there may be enough loss of your mental alertness, vigilance, and timing that you will be at a real disadvantage in tending to serious business for the next few days. You certainly should not attempt intricate physical or mental tasks the day after your long trip over many time zones.

The whole problem relates to the body's loss of the synchronization among various natural body rhythms within the time zone in which you arrive. Your body has multiple rhythms including wakefulness and sleep, hormone secretion, bowel elimination, appetite, etc. which normally revolve around a 24 to 25 hour interval. If you change the outside time, your body tries to reset your inward rhythms to match the new periods of light/dark and awake/sleep. Because of fast travel across multiple time zones, your body is unable to resynchronize your rhythms quickly, and it takes about one day for each time zone crossed for you to get back in step. Most people find that westward travel is easier to handle than eastward travel, probably because the body's natural rhythm interval of about 25 hours can be more easily stretched to the longer day encountered as you go westward, than it can be compressed to fit the shorter day in going eastward.

The best way to handle jet-lag is to go to sleep at the usual local time, around 10:00 or 11:00 p.m. You may need to go to bed before you are really ready to retire on an eastward flight, and you may need to make yourself stay awake longer than you would prefer to do on a westward flight. If you fly overnight eastward, as from New York to London, you should try to sleep on the flight, even if that flight is from 8:00 p.m. to 2:00 a.m. New York time, so that when you arrive in the morning, you will be able to stay awake the next day. The easiest way to get to sleep, and to stay asleep a reasonable period each night after you arrive in your new time zone may be to take a short-acting hypnotic for the first couple of nights until your body rhythms are more in adjustment. It may be necessary for you to keep taking it for four to eight nights, depending upon how far you have traveled and how susceptible you are (50). Again, it is important to take any prescription drug only under a physician's advice, particularly these types of drugs.

Attempts to prevent jet-lag have been popularized, in particular the Argonne Anti-Jet-Lag-Diet described by Dr. C. F. Ehret, a scientist working at the U.S. Department of Energy's Argonne National Laboratory in Illinois. His diet is a feast-fast-feast-fast program started three days before your departure, with feast days of high protein breakfasts and lunches, and high carbohydrate dinners alternated with fast days of fruit and "skimpy" salads. Despite its popularity—a diet even used, it is said, by President Reagan—there is absolutely no published evidence that it works, and there is absolutely no scientific rationale to explain why it should work. After being taken in by what sounded like an official U.S. government approved program, we found the diet to be worthless, and most probably, you will too. However, do not be surprised if you get some effect, because there is a lot of psychology in jet-lag. Witness most people's lesser trouble when they arrive at their vacation destination, than when they return home. The excitement of London, Paris, or Timbuktu possibly will cover up much of what your body is going through. If, like Dorothy in the "Wizard of Oz," you really believe the Argonne diet will help, it probably will—but that is because you really believed it would!

Serious scientific work is going on concerning ways to alter your sleep-inducing hormones, including one hormone that responds to light, called melatonin. Despite some encouraging preliminary reports with melatonin, and with variable times of a person's exposure to sunlight, the situation remains as it was: there is no practical way to prevent your jet-lag, but there is fairly good relief in short-acting hypnotic drugs until your body rhythms catch up.

Obvious ways to prevent jet-lag include taking a slower boat, train, or bus, and allowing your body to adjust as you cross about one time-zone a day. If you have the time, a ship is a great way for you to cross oceans and to arrive feeling relaxed. The only problem is that on most cruises, you will probably arrive six pounds heavier. We are delighted that at least two cruise lines—Royal and Cunard—are providing alternative "healthy" diets and excellent work-out space on their boats. With them, you can take a slow boat, relax, not worry about jet-lag and not destroy your healthy life-style.

Problems with Gas

Air taken up to 6,000 feet, the atmospheric level present within most plane cabins, will expand its volume by about 30% if it is free to do so, because of the lower atmospheric pressure. This is not a problem, unless the air is in your ears, gut, or other contained spaces where it is not free to expand. Again, usually there is no problem, except that you may notice a bit more bowel gas, and you may need to "clear" or to "pop" your ears during ascent or descent in maintaining equal pressure against your ear drums. That is a good reason not to sleep during either ascent or descent.

Some people, however, may experience more trouble from the expanding body gases. Babies who do not know how to "clear," and sufferers from inflammation of the ears (otitis) or the sinuses (sinusitis) may experience considerable ear discomfort. Fortunately, the air passages in babies are straighter and are more easily kept open, so babies rarely have ear pain. If you have an upper respiratory infection (a cold or flu), take a decongestant and use long-lasting nose drops before you go on board. People who have had surgery recently may experience discomfort from expanded gas in the gut or chest. A particular problem may occur when a person travels by air soon after a plaster cast has been put on his or her broken leg—a common problem for all those Texans skiing in Colorado. Air trapped within the cast may expand and cause acute discomfort to swollen tissues. So, casts may need to be split before the person undertakes a long flight.

Ozone

Flying high in the sky will increase your exposure to ozone—the atmospheric component that protects us on the ground against dangerous ultraviolet radiation—ozone that is rapidly being depleted in our use of fire extinguishers, hair sprays, and other aerosols containing hydrocarbons. The traveler's short-term increased exposure to ozone at 40,000 feet is possibly irrelevant, but the depletion of the ozone layer by man-made chemicals could lead to marked increases in skin cancer, including malignant melanoma. There are even more serious consequences to fish life and to overall food production which could also follow. So, the recent attention to this problem is certainly appropriate.

Preventing Motion Sickness

Few discomforts are as bad as motion sickness. First you feel as if you are going to die; then you wish you could. But take heart: the more you fly, the less likely you will be to develop motion sickness. And, with today's faster and sleeker jets that can fly high enough for you to escape turbulence, motion sickness seems to be less of a problem. Also, there are more effective preventatives, the most widely used being a skin-patch that delivers a small amount of the drug scopolamine for up to three days. However, it is seldom that you would use such preventative measures, unless you are prone to becoming air-sick even during non-turbulent flights, or you know turbulent air will be encountered. More likely, you will not expect to become air-sick, and therefore, you will not use the preventative medication. However, before a long boat trip, particularly when heavy seas are ahead of you, you can use such medication enough ahead of time to be of help. There is some rather weak evidence that powdered ginger root may prevent the problem, but where in the world are you going to find some, unless you are flying Japan Air and sushi is served with pickled ginger?

Therefore, just hope your flight does not encounter the type of turbulence that will bring on motion sickness. If you start feeling queasy, nauseated, pale and sweaty, try to relax, lie back quietly, shut your eyes, and take a few deep breaths—but not too many or you will hyperventilate. There is a lot of anxiety involved in motion sickness. Once one person begins to vomit, there may be a ripple effect through the nearby passengers.

Altitude Sickness

You should not suffer from the 5,000 to 6,000 feet atmospheric pressure within the airplane cabin. But within three to six hours after you arrive in Sante Fe, in Aspen, in Mexico City or in other places over 7,000 feet, you may very well get a headache, become breathless, woozy and lethargic, and hardly able to move about. Sleep may be difficult the first night, and you may still feel headachy and lethargic the next day, unable to ski well or to do whatever else brought you to such high places. After that, you will probably regain your composure, but you will have suffered acute altitude or mountain sickness (51).

These symptoms are related to the body's natural reaction to the lower amount of oxygen available at heights much above 7,000 feet. The reaction involves an increased rate and depth of breathing—the same old hyperventilation. Under these circumstances though, the hyperventilation is needed. Unfortunately, the overbreathing removes so much of the acidic carbon dioxide from the lungs that the body fluids become more alkaline, the process being called acute respiratory alkalosis.

This alkaline state, in turn, slows down the overbreathing which restricts oxygen and causes the symptoms of altitude sickness.

The problem is more common with rapid ascent to fairly high places, such as is possible with air travel today, compared to the time when it took days to get up to so high an altitude and during which the body had time to acclimate. Mountain climbers who climb to very high altitudes are still threatened by the altitude, and they may actually develop much more serious troubles than the typically mild symptoms most people develop between 7,000 and 12,000 feet.

Altitude sickness can usually be prevented by use of the drug, acetazolamide (Diamox), a weak diuretic that also acts to make the body fluids more acidic (52). That process overcomes the effect of the alkaline state, so that you can hyperventilate appropriately. If you take 500 mg. of Diamox the day before you travel and again the day you reach high altitude, most likely you will escape the headache and the other symptoms of mountain sickness. The Diamox may cause a tingly sensation in your hands and feet, a flat taste to carbonated beverages, and a little increase in urination, but most people find its side effects to be much less of a bother than what it prevents.

There are other ways to prevent mountain sickness, including the use of adrenal steroids (53), but Diamox is the easiest drug for most travelers to use at moderately high altitudes.

Other Discomforts of Travel

This book is not intended to cover all of the problems of traveling beyond the U.S.A. Some of the more exotic foreign destinations have some special exotic problems, including the need to protect yourself from yellow fever by immunizations, and from malaria by drugs. If you need such advice and you cannot get it from your travel agent, obtain *Health Information for International Travel* from the U.S. Government Printing Office, Washington, D.C. 20402.

Traveler's diarrhea is more of a problem when you travel outside the U.S.A., but the strange foods and drinks you consume when you are away from home may upset your GI tract, even in Miami or Los Angeles. There is no need for you to take anti-diarrhea pills before traveling within the U.S., but if diarrhea begins, immediately start using Pepto-Bismol or Kaopectate, and if the trots turn into more persistent trouble, take the prescription drugs, Imodium or Lomotil.

Problems for Those Already Sick

If you are in bad health already, flying may add another burden to your cardiovascular system. Commercial aircraft cabins are pressurized to between 5,000 and 6,000 feet, even though, if you are one of the fortunate few, you may be flying on a Concorde at 60,000 feet. At this cabin altitude, the pressure of oxygen in the air falls by about thirty percent. Fortunately, the amount of oxygen in your blood, because of the special protection provided by our oxygen carrying system, falls only about three percent. That little fall in oxygenation, which accompanies the usual atmospheric pressure in aircraft cabins, is perfectly comfortable for most of us, except that the dryness of the compressed external air, blown into the cabin to keep the pressure up, may be a problem for some people with sensitive skin, eyes, or throats.

However, for some individuals with underlying diseases, even that atmospheric level—about where the residents of Denver live—may be a problem, mainly because the exposure develops over a very short time, and we cannot compensate for it, and because those with heart or lung disease may not be able to compensate.

These guidelines should be followed for people with the following diseases (51):

- Pulmonary: if you become short of breath after walking a block on level ground, most likely you will need extra oxygen during your flight. Asthma should not be a problem. If you have lots of sputum, it may be more difficult to bring it up.
- Cardiac: if you can handle ten stairs without pain or shortness of breath, most likely you will tolerate flight. If you have recently had a heart attack, ask your doctor, because the results of a stress test can fairly well predict whether or not you will have trouble in-flight.
- Severe anemia: rarely a problem. Sickle cell patients very rarely need extra oxygen.
- Neurological: those who have recently had a stroke may become confused. Epilepsy will break through medication very rarely, so that an extra dose may be needed before long flights.

All of these people and others who are ill are particularly advised to stay away from cigarette smoke and alcohol during flight—the smoke because it will further reduce their oxygen supply, the alcohol because it will depress their brain functions.

The symptoms of too little oxygen (hypoxia) usually start with an individual's subtle personality change, coupled with a "high" feeling (euphoria). Thereafter, the person's judgment becomes impaired, memory is lost, and coordination falters. These symptoms seem to resemble the early stages of alcoholic intoxication, but if you feel them without having had anything to drink, you should reach for the oxygen. Unfortunately, the symptoms of alcoholic intoxication are not relieved by oxygen, but putting the oxygen mask on the obnoxious drunk in the next seat may be a way to shut him up.

When you have had too little oxygen, you breathe faster and deeper to try to overcome the oxygen lack. Unfortunately, that may lead to further trouble because the symptoms of overbreathing or hyperventilation which are caused by blowing off too much carbon dioxide. These symptoms include feeling light-headed and floaty, experiencing anxiety, numbness, and tingling in the fingers, feeling a fast heart beat, seeing spots before the eyes, and hearing ringing in the ear. If these symptoms seem familiar, realize that whenever you are stressed, you may hyperventilate, obviously without any lack of oxygen being responsible.

Problems for the Disabled

Because about one out of five people over age fifteen, almost 35 million Americans, has some physical impairment, there is an obvious need for them to ease their way through the barriers of travel. Many carriers and hotels are making some progress in providing room for wheelchairs, removable armrests, and accessible lavatories, but the disabled traveler must still find out beforehand what is available and make plans accordingly. Air travel is best without the need to transfer, particularly at small airports, and there are some new airplanes, such as Boeing 767s, which have lavatories designed for wheelchairs. Some travel agents specialize in assisting the disabled, including these listed in *The New York Times* of 30 Aug. 1987:

Accessible Tours
344 Main Street
Mount Kisco, NY 10549
914-241-1700

A-1 Cruise and Travel Center
Post Office Box 3800
Apollo Beach, FL 33570
813-645-6699

Canwee Travel
553 Broadway
Massapequa, NY 11758
516-798-7171

Evergreen Travel Service
19505 44th Avenue West
Lynnwood, WA 98036
206-776-1184

Flying Wheels Travel
143 West Bridge Street
Post Office Box 382
Owatonna, MN 55060
507-451-5005

Whole Person Tours
Post Office Box 1084
Bayonne, NJ 07002
201-858-3400

Detailed information is available from these sources:

- "Travel for the Disabled," published by Twin Peaks Press, Portland, Oregon.
- "Questions and Answers about Air Travel for the Wheelchair User" from Eastern Paralyzed Veterans Association, 432 Park Avenue South, New York, New York 10016.
- "Directory of Aircraft Facilities for Disabled People" (information on the 41 carriers flying into Britain) from Access to Skies, 25 Mortimer St., London W1N 8AB, England.
- "The Handicapped Driver's Mobility Guide," by the American Automobile Association's Traffic Safety Department, 8111 Gatehouse Road, Falls Church, VA 22047.
- Information about cruise ships from Mr. Tom Gilbert, Travel Industry and Disabled Exchange, P.O. Box 15777, Tampa, FL 33684.

One way or another, many disabled people can join the mob of travelers across the U.S. That way, they too can enjoy the delays at the airports, the lost luggage, and the taxi rides into Manhattan, but they can also experience the many real pleasures and opportunities of travel in the U.S.A. and Canada.

Chapter 4
Choices After You Arrive: Restaurants And Hotels That Provide Healthy Choices In The Largest Cities In The United States And Canada

Once you have survived the exigencies of travel, including the cab ride down the minefield known as FDR Drive, or the shooting gallery known as the Santa Monica Freeway, you are ready for a hot shower, a cool drink, exciting cuisine, and relaxing sleep. If you plan your moves adroitly, these indulgences can be yours, getting you in top shape for the next day's appointments.

The plans revolve around two major choices: where you will stay and where will you eat. This chapter is designed to help you make these two choices in the best way, both for your short-term comfort and for your longtime good health. We have taken the forty-four largest metropolitan areas in the U.S. and Canada, and distilling what is available from various sources, we have listed the hotels that will allow you to stay in good shape and the restaurants that will help you to keep your weight, cholesterol and blood pressure down. Our lists are not intended to be all inclusive. We only aim to provide you with a reasonably large and varied selection, most of the hotels being within the central city areas or near the airport.

In addition to a significant amount of our personal sampling, the sources of our hotel listings include a large number of general guidebooks, including the two best ones for the traveler— *Birnbaum's USA 1988 for Business Travelers* (Houghton Mufflin: Boston, 1987) and Rand McNally's *Business Traveler's City Guide* (Rand McNally: Chicago, 1988). We have also gone over two books listing exercise facilities: John Winsor's *Fitness on the Road* (Shelter Publications: Bolinas, California, 1986) and *The NESRA Traveler's Fitness/Health Directory* (Lake County Press: Waukegan, Illinois, 1985).

We have focused on those exercise facilities which are the most popular and the most sensible for the usual traveler: workout facilities (usually stationary bikes, treadmills, and Nautilus-type equipment), jogging tracks, and swimming pools. Almost all the facilities listed have workout facilities with pools, and these pools need to be on the grounds of the hotel, not "available nearby"—because that often may mean the "Y" which is two miles away. It is hard enough to make yourself exercise when you are on the road, so do not put additional obstacles in the way because they can easily be used as an excuse.

We have not paid attention to the tariff, because it will not vary that much, or we assume that you are on the expense account. If you are looking for more moderate prices, consider the Marriott's Courtyard Hotels. They offer large rooms, and they have swimming pools and exercise rooms.

Joggers don't live longer, it just seems like it.
—Anonymous

One general class of hotels deserves your special attention: those hotels that have all suites, such as the Embassy, Guest Quarters, or Residence Inns. Not only are these hotels often less expensive than traditional hotels, but also they provide more room, usually with kitchen facilities. Many have workout rooms, but fewer of them have pools. Although these hotels now make up only about 2% of U.S. hotel rooms, they will grow to 7% of the total within five years. If you are going to stay in one place for more than a couple of days, and particularly, if you have lots of paper work to do, rooms at an all-suite hotel would make it easier to prepare some of your own (nutritious) meals and would leave you more time for work.

In the restaurant selections derived from our extensive travels, we have added the recommendations of food editors from the major metropolitan newspapers, the city magazines, and from the selections of the local affiliates of the American Heart Association (AHA) whose personnel have found out which restaurants routinely, or at your request, will prepare items according to the AHA's dietary guidelines. The AHA Dining Out Program licenses restaurants to use the AHA logo, with the identifying phrases—"Eating Away From Home" or "Creative Cuisine"—if the restaurant agrees to these criteria:

- No more than five grams of fat per ounce of meat, fish, or poultry entrées.
- No more than six ounces cooked weight for entrées.
- Cook by baking, broiling, poaching, or grilling with minimal amounts of unsaturated vegetable oils.
- Restrict high cholesterol/high fat foods such as egg yolks and whole milk.
- Use non-sodium flavorings to keep the sodium content for an entrée to below 500-800 milligrams.

The guidelines also encourage the availability of fruit for dessert and the availability of non-smoking areas for guests.

*Guilt is nothing more than repressed anger over the
small portions served in expensive restaurants.*
—Richard Smith

Foods which fall under the AHA guidelines are, obviously, healthier for you, and we are delighted to report that over thirty of the AHA
affiliates have either already published their local area Dining Guide
(available from the local AHA office) or are preparing one. The Guide
is an idea that will continue to spread and one which will help all of us to
find the right stuff when we go out to eat.

Our listing especially stresses restaurants that provide seafood,
Mediterranean, Japanese, and "nouvelle" cuisine. For additional information you should read the AHA's booklet, *Dining Out,* available
from your local AHA affiliate. As with the hotels, we have not been
overly concerned about a restaurant's location or price because that
is something you can easily check by phone before you go out. We
have included some of the 5-star gourmet places, as well as some of
the trendy, less-expensive ones in every city. The prices for the
restaurants are: inexpensive - less than $15 per person; moderate - up
to $25 per person; and expensive - more than $40 per person (all
prices not including tax, tip or drinks). In cities such as New York, Los
Angeles and Chicago, there are many more suitable restaurants than
we have listed. Our selections, at least, provide you with a number of
attractive choices at varying price ranges. Because some of the
"healthier" choices may be new, you had better check to see whether
or not they are still open, as restaurants often come and go quickly in
the big cities.

*On nouvelle cuisine: It's so beautifully arranged on the
plate you know someone's fingers have been all over
it.—Julia Child*

So, traveler, choose your hotel for healthy living, and your restaurants for healthy eating from the following lists—and enjoy your time
away from home.

Hotels in the forty largest U.S. and the four largest Canadian
cities are listed first. Then come the restaurants in the same forty-four
cities.

HOTEL	Work-out	Jogging	Swimming
United States			
Albuquerque, NM			
Amberley Suites I-25 and San Francisco Rd S 505/823-1300	●		●
Amfac 2910 Yale Blvd. SE 505/823-7000	●		●
Hilton Inn 1901 University Blvd. NE 505/884-2500	●	●	●
Marriott 2101 Louisiana Blvd. NE 505/881-6800	●	●	●
Sheraton-Old Town 800 Rio Grande Blvd. NW 505/843-6300	●		●
Santa Fe, NM			
Bishop's Lodge Bishop's Lodge Road 505/983-6377		●	●
La Posada 330 E. Palace 505/983-6351			
Rancho Encantado Tesuque, Rt. 22 505/982-3537		●	●
Sheraton Inn 750 N. St. Francis 505/982-5591	●		●
Atlanta, GA			
Colony Square Peachtree & 14th St. 404/892-6000	●		●
Falcon Inn and Conference Center Suanee Road at I-85 (Norcross) 404/945-6751	●		●

HOTEL	Work-out	Jogging	Swimming
Hilton & Towers Courtland & Harris N.E. 404/659-2000	●	●	●
Hyatt Regency 265 Peachtree N.E. 404/577-1234	●		●
Airport Marriott 4711 Best Road 404/766-7900	●	●	
Marriott Marquis 265 Peachtree Center Ave 404/521-0000	●		●
Marriott NW 200 Interstate N. Pkwy. 404/952-7900	●	●	●
Omni Int'l Hotel One Omni International N.W. 404/659-0000	●		●
Peachtree Plaza Peachtree at International 404/659-1400	●		●
Ritz-Carlton - Buckhead 3434 Peachtree 404/637-2700	●		●
Sheraton Century Center 2000 Century Blvd., N.E. 404/325-0000	●	●	●
Westin Peachtree Plaza 210 Peachtree St. 404/659-1400	●	●	●
Baltimore, MD			
Belvedere Charles St. at Chase St. 1 E. Chase Street 301/332-1000	●		●
Cross Keys Inn 5100 Falls Rd. 301/532-6900	●	●	●

HOTEL	Work-out	Jogging	Swimming
Marriott-Inner Harbor Pratt & Eutaw Sts. 301/962-0202	●		●
Hyatt Regency-Inner Harbor 300 Light St. 301/528-1234	●	●	●
Omni International Hotel 101 W. Fayette St. 301/752-1100	●		●
Sheraton Inner Harbor Hotel 300 S. Charles St. 301/962-8300	●		●

Boston, MA

HOTEL	Work-out	Jogging	Swimming
Four Seasons 200 Boylston St. 617/338-4400	●		●
Hyatt Regency Cambridge 575 Memorial Dr. (Cambridge) 617/492-1234	●		●
Marriott in Copley Place 110 Huntington Avenue 617/236-5800	●		●
Marriott Long Wharf 296 State St. 617/227-0800	●		●
Marriott Newton 2345 Commonwealth Ave. (Newton) 617/969-1000	●		●
Le Meridien Hotel 250 Franklin St. 617/451-1900	●		●
Royal Sonesta 5 Cambridge Pkwy. (Cambridge) 617/491-3600	●		●
Sheraton Mansfield Inn 31 Hampshire St. (Mansfield) 617/339-2200	●		●

HOTEL	Work-out	Jogging	Swimming
Sheraton Rolling Green Inn 311 Lowell St. (Andover) 617/475-5400	●	●	●
Sheraton Towers Hotel 39 Dalton St. 617/236-2000	●	●	
Westin Hotel, Copley Place 10 Huntington Ave. 617/262-9600	●	●	●

Chicago, IL

HOTEL	Work-out	Jogging	Swimming
Drake Oakbrook Hotel 2301 York Rd. (Oak Brook) 312/574-5700		●	●
Hilton Arlington Park 3400 W. Euclid Ave. 312/394-2000	●	●	●
Hilton and Towers 720 S. Michigan 312/922-4400	●	●	●
Holiday Inn City Centre 300 E. Ohio 312/787-6100	●		●
Hyatt Regency O'Hare 9300 W. Bryn Mawr 312/696-1234	●		●
Marriott 540 N. Michigan Ave. 312/836-0100	●	●	●
Marriott O'Hare 8535 West Higgins Rd. 312/693-4444	●		●
McCormick Center Hotel 23rd & Lake Shore Dr. 312/791-1900	●		●
Palmer House Towers 17 E. Monroe St. 312/726-7500	●		●

HOTEL	Work-out	Jogging	Swimming
Ritz-Carlton 160 E. Pearson St. at Water Tower Pl. 312/266-1000	●		●
Westin Chicago 909 N. Michigan Ave. 312/943-7200	●	●	
Westin O'Hare 6100 River Road 312/698-6000	●		●

Cincinnati, OH

HOTEL	Work-out	Jogging	Swimming
Clarion 141 West 6th St. 513/352-2100	●		●
Drawbridge Inn I-75 and Buttermilk Pk. (Fort Mitchell) 606/341-2800		●	●
Hartley Hotel 8020 Montgomery Rd. 513/793-4300	●		●
Hyatt Regency 151 W. 5th St. 513/579-1234	●		●
Marriott 11320 Chester Rd. (Sharonville) 513/772-1720	●		●
Omni Netherland Plaza 35 W. 5th St. 513/421-9100	●		●
Sheraton Springdale 11911 Sheraton Ln. 513/671-6600		●	●
Westin 500 Vine St. 513/621-7700	●		●

Cleveland, OH

HOTEL	Work-out	Jogging	Swimming
Bond Court Hotel 777 St. Clair 216/771-7600	●	●	●
Harley Hotel of Cleveland South 5300 Rockside Rd. (Independence) 216/524-0700	●		●
Harley Hotel West 17000 Bagley Rd. (Middleburg Heights) 216/243-5200	●		●
Hilton Inn/South 6100 Rockside Rd. 216/524-8050		●	●
Holiday Inn 1100 Crocker Rd. (Westlake) 216/871-6500		●	●
Holiday Inn - Coliseum 4742 Brecksville Rd. (Richfield) 216/659-6151	●		●
Holiday Inn-Lakeside City Center Lakeside & E-12th St. 216/241-5100	●		●
Hollenden House Hotel 610 Superior 216/621-0700	●		●
Marriott East 3663 Park East Dr. 216/464-5950	●		●
Sheraton Hopkins Airport 5300 Riverside Drive 216/267-1500	●		●
Stouffer's Inn 24 Public Square 216/696-5600	●	●	●

HOTEL

Dallas, TX

Hotel	Work-out	Jogging	Swimming
Adolphus 1321 Commerce St 214/742-8200	●		
Doubletree, Lincoln Center 5410 L.B.J. Frwy. 214/934-8400	●	●	●
Grand Kempinski 15201 Dallas Pkwy. 214/386-6000	●	●	●
Holiday Inn Brookhollow 7050 N. Stemmons Frwy. 214/630-8500	●		●
Holiday Inn/Crowne Plaza 4099 Valley View 214/385-9000	●	●	●
Hyatt Regency DFW Airport International Pkwy. 214/453-8400	●		●
Hyatt Regency Dallas 300 Reunion Blvd. 214/651-1234	●	●	●
Loews Anatole 2201 Stemmons Frwy. 214/748-1200	●	●	●
Marriott Hotel Mandalay at Las Colinas 221 S. Las Colinas Blvd. 214/556-0800	●		●
Marriott Quorum 14901 Dallas Pkwy. 214/661-2800	●		●
Marriott D/FW Airport 8440 Freeport Pkwy. 214/929-8800	●		●
Plaza of the Americas 650 N. Pearl St. 214/979-9000	●	●	

HOTEL

Hotel	Work-out	Jogging	Swimming
Sheraton Dallas 400 N. Olive 214/922-8000	●	●	
Sheraton Grand D/FW Airport Esters Blvd. & Hwy. 114 (Irving) 214/929-8400	●	●	●
Sheraton-Park Central 12720 Merit Dr. 214/385-3000	●	●	●
Westin Galleria 13340 Dallas N. Pkwy. 214/934-9494	●	●	●
Stouffer 2222 N. Stemmons Pkwy. 214/631-2222	●	●	●

Denver, CO

Hotel	Work-out	Jogging	Swimming
Brown Palace 321 17th St. 303/297-3111	●		
Executive Tower Inn 1405 Curtis St. 303/571-0300	●	●	●
Holiday Inn SE-Tech Center I-25 at Arapahoe Rd. Exit 9009 E. Arapahoe (Englewood) 303/790-1421	●		●
Hyatt Regency 1750 Welton St. 303/295-1200		●	●
Oxford Alexis 1600 17th St. 303/628-5400	●	●	
Raffles Hotel-Southeast 3200 South Parker Rd. 303/695-1700	●	●	●
Regency Hotel 3900 Elati St. 303/458-0808	●		●

HOTEL	Work-out	Jogging	Swimming
Sheraton-Tech Center 4900 DTC Pkwy. 303/779-1100	●		●
Sheraton Inn-Lakewood 360 Union Blvd. (Lakewood) 303/987-2000	●	●	●
Stapleton Plaza 3333 Quebec St. 303/321-3500	●	●	
Westin, Tabor Center 1672 Lawrence St 303/572-9100	●		●
Writer's Manor Hotel 1730 S. Colorado Blvd. 303/756-8877		●	●

Detroit, MI

HOTEL	Work-out	Jogging	Swimming
Dearborn Towne House Motel 2101 S. Telegraph (Dearborn) 313/274-5700	●	●	●
Hilton Inn Airport 31500 Wick Rd. 313/292-3400	●		●
Holiday Inn-Livonia West 17123 Laurel Pk. Dr. (Liviona) 313/464-1300	●		●
Michigan Inn 16400 J.L. Hudson Dr. (Southfield) 313/559-6500	●		●
Omni International 333 E. Jefferson 313/222-7700	●		
Ramada Inn-Metropolitan Airport 8270 Wickham 313/729-6300	●		●

HOTEL	Work-out	Jogging	Swimming
Sheraton Oaks 27000 Sheraton Dr. (Novi) 313/348-5000	●		●
Westin-Renaissance Center Renaissance Center 313/568-8000	●	●	●

Honolulu, HI

HOTEL	Work-out	Jogging	Swimming
Kahala Hilton 5000 Kahala Ave 808/734-2211	●		●
Ilikai Hotel 1777 AlaMoana Blvd. 808/949-3811		●	●
New Otani-Kaimana Beach 2863 Kalakaua Ave 808/923-1555		●	●

Houston, TX

HOTEL	Work-out	Jogging	Swimming
Adam's Mark 2900 Briar Park Dr. 713/978-7400	●		●
Allen Park Inn 2121 Allen Parkway 800/231-6310 & 713/521-9321	●	●	●
Embassy Suite 9090 Southwest Frwy. 713/995-0123	●		●
Four Season Hotel 1300 Lamar St. 713/650-1300	●		●
Holiday Inn - Intercontinental 3702 North Belt 713/449-2311	●	●	●
Houstonian 111 N. Post Oak Ln. 713/680-2626	●	●	●
Inn on the Park Four Riverway at Loop 610 713/871-8181	●	●	●

HOTEL	Work-out	Jogging	Swimming
Inter-Continental 5150 Westheimer 713/961-1500	●		●
Marriott-Greens Point 255 N. Belt Dr. 713/875-4000	●		●
Sheraton Crown- Intercontinental 15700 Drummet 713/442-5100	●		●
Westin Galleria 5060 W. Alabama 713/960-8100	●	●	●
Westin Oaks 5011 Westheimer 713/623-4300	●	●	●

Indianapolis, IN

HOTEL	Work-out	Jogging	Swimming
Adam's Mark 2544 Executive Drive 317/248-2481	●		●
Hilton Inn-Airport 2500 High School Road 317/244-3361	●	●	●
Holiday Inn South 520 E. Thompson 317/787-8341	●	●	●
Marriott Hotel 7202 E. 21st St. 317/352-1231	●		●
Radisson Plaza 8787 Keystone Crossing 317/846-2700	●	●	●
Riverpointe Suites Executel 1150 N. White River Pkwy. W. Dr. 317/638-9866	●	●	●
Sheraton Meridian 2820 N. Meridian St. 317/924-1241	●		●

HOTEL	Work-out	Jogging	Swimming
Sheraton Marten House 1801 W. 86th St. 317/872-4111	●		●

Jacksonville, FL

HOTEL	Work-out	Jogging	Swimming
Best Western Inn 5221 University Blvd W 904/737-1690	●		●
Holiday Inn-Airport Airport Road at I-95 904/757-3110	●		●
Holiday Inn-Orange Park I-295 at US 17 (Orange Park) 904/264-9513	●		●
Park Suite 9300 Baymeadows Rd. 904/731-3555	●		●
Sheraton-St John's Place 1515 Prudential Dr. 904/396-5100	●	●	●

Kansas City, MO & KS

HOTEL	Work-out	Jogging	Swimming
Adam's Mark 9103 E. 39th St. 816/737-0200	●		●
Alameda Plaza Wornall Rd. and Ward Pkwy. 816/756-1500	●	●	●
Doubletree-Corporate Woods 10100 College Blvd. (Overland Park) 913/451-6100		●	●
Hilton Inn-Airport 112th St. N.W. & I-29 816/891-8900	●	●	●
Howard Johnson 1600 NE Parvin Rd. 816/453-5210	●		●

HOTEL	Work-out	Jogging	Swimming
Hyatt Regency-Crown Center 2345 McGee 816/421-1234	●		●
Marriott-Overland Park 10800 Melcalf Ave. (Overland Park) 913/451-8000	●		●
Park Place Hotel 1601 N. Universal Ave. 816/483-9900	●	●	●
Residence Inn 6300 W. 110th St. (Overland Park) 913/491-3333	●		●
Sheraton Airport 7301 N.W. Tiffany Springs 816/741-9500	●		●
Vista International 200 West 12th St. 816/421-6800	●	●	●
Westin-Crown Center One Pershing Rd. 816/474-4400	●	●	●

Las Vegas, NV

HOTEL	Work-out	Jogging	Swimming
Aladdin 3667 Las Vegas Blvd. 702/736-0111	●		●
Bally's Las Vegas 3645 Las Vegas Blvd. S. 702/739-4111	●		●
Caesar's Palace 3570 Las Vegas Blvd. S. 702/731-7110	●		●
Golden Nugget 129 E. Fremont St. 702/385-7111	●		●
Hilton-Flamingo 3555 Las Vegas Blvd. S. 702/733-3111	●		●

HOTEL	Work-out	Jogging	Swimming
Holiday Inn 3475 Las Vegas Blvd. S. 702/369-5000	●		●
Sahara 2535 Las Vegas Blvd. S. 702/737-2111	●		●
Sands 3355 Las Vegas Blvd. S. 702/733-5000	●	●	●

Los Angeles, CA

HOTEL	Work-out	Jogging	Swimming
Ambassador Garden 3400 Wilshire Blvd 800/421-0182 & 213/387-7011	●	●	●
Beverly Plaza 8384 W. 3rd St. 213/658-6600	●		●
Beverly Wilshire 9500 Wilshire Blvd (Beverly Hills) 213/275-4282	●		●
Century Plaza 2025 Avenue of the Stars 213/277-2000	●	●	●
Hilton-Los Angeles Airport 5711 West Century Blvd. 213/410-4000	●	●	
Hyatt Los Angeles Airport 6225 W. Century Blvd. 213/670-9000	●	●	●
Le Parc Hotel 733 N. West Knoll (West Hollywood) 213/855-8888	●	●	●
Marina City Club 4333 Admiralty Way (Marina Del Rey) 213/822-0611	●	●	●

HOTEL	Work-out	Jogging	Swimming
Mondrian Hotel 8440 Sunset Blvd. (West Hollywood) 213/650-8999	●		●
New Otani 120 S. Los Angeles St. 213/629-1200	●		
Sheraton Grande 333 S. Figueroa St. 213/671-1133	●		●
Sheraton Plaza La Reina (Airport) 6101 W. Century Blvd. 213/642-1111	●		●
Sheraton Universal 333 Universal Terrace Pkwy. (Universal City) 818/980-1212	●		●
Westin Bonaventure 404 S. Figueroa St. 213/624-1000	●	●	●
Westwood Marquis 930 Hilgard Ave. (Westwood Village) 213/208-8765	●		●

Louisville, KY

HOTEL	Work-out	Jogging	Swimming
Breckinridge Inn Breckinridge Lane and Watterson Expressway 502/456-5050	●		●
Brown 4th and Broadway 502/583-1234	●		
Galt House 4th Ave. at River Rd. 502/589-5200	●		●
Hyatt Regency 320 W. Jefferson 502/587-3434	●		●

HOTEL	Work-out	Jogging	Swimming
Ramada Inn East 9700 Bluegrass Pkwy. 502/491-4830			●
Seelbach Hotel 500 4th Ave. 502/585-3200		●	
Sheraton Lakeview I-65 and Stansifer Ave. (Clarksville) 812/283-4411	●		●

Memphis, TN

HOTEL	Work-out	Jogging	Swimming
Coach & Four 1318 Lamar Ave. 901/726-5000	●		●
Holiday Inn Crowne Plaza 250 N. Main 901/527-7300	●		●
Hyatt Regency-Ridgeway 939 Ridge Lake Blvd. 901/761-1234	●	●	●
Peabody 149 Union Ave. 901/529-4000	●		●
Radisson 185 Union Ave. 901/528-1800	●		●

Miami, FL

HOTEL	Work-out	Jogging	Swimming
Castle Premier 5445 Collins Ave. (Miami Beach) 305/865-1500	●		●
Doral on the Ocean 4833 Collins Ave. (Miami Beach) 800/327-6334 & 305/532-3600	●	●	●
Four Ambassador 801 S.E. Bayshore Dr. 305/377-1966	●		●

HOTEL	Work-out	Jogging	Swimming
Grand Bay Shore 2669 S. Bayshore Dr. 305/858-9600	●		●
Hilton-Fontainebleu 4441 Collins Ave. 305/538-2000	●		●
Hilton-Miami Airport 5101 Blue Lagoon Dr. 305/262-1000	●	●	●
Inter-Continental 100 Chopin Plaza 305/577-1000		●	●
Marriott-Miami Airport 1201 N.W. LeJeune 305/649-5000		●	●
Plaza Venetia 555 NE 15th St. 305/374-2900	●	●	●
Radisson Mart Plaza 711 N.W. 72 Ave. 305/261-3800	●	●	●
Sheraton Bal Harbour 9701 Collins Ave. 305/865-7511	●	●	●
Sheraton Riverhouse (Airport) 3900 N.W. 21st St. 305/871-3800	●	●	●
Sonesta Beach 350 Ocean Dr. (Key Biscayne) 305/361-2021	●		●

Milwaukee, WI

HOTEL	Work-out	Jogging	Swimming
Astor Hotel 924 E. Juneau Ave. 414/271-4220		●	
Holiday Inn South-Airport 6331 S. 13th St. 414/764-1500	●	●	

HOTEL	Work-out	Jogging	Swimming
Marc Plaza 509 W. Wisconsin Ave. 414/271-7250	●		●
Pfister 424 E. Wisconsin Ave. 414/273-8222	●		●

Minneapolis/St. Paul, MN

HOTEL	Work-out	Jogging	Swimming
Holiday Inn North 1501 Freeway Blvd. (Brooklyn Center) 612/566-4140	●		●
Holiday Inn St. Paul/East 2201 Burns Ave. 612/731-2220	●		●
Hyatt Regency-Minneapolis 1300 Nicollet Mall 612/370-1234	●	●	●
Marriott at City Center 30 S. 7th St. Mpls. 612/349-4000	●		
Ramada-St. Paul 1870 Old Hudson Rd. 612/735-2330	●		●
Ritz Hotel-Minneapolis 315 Nicollet Mall 612/332-4000	●		●
Sheraton Airport 2525 E. 78th St. 612/854-1771	●		●
Sheraton Park Place- Minneapolis 5555 Wayzata Blvd. 612/542-8600	●	●	●

HOTEL

Nashville, TN

Hotel	Work-out	Jogging	Swimming
Doubletree 2 Commerce Place 615/244-8200	●		●
Holiday Inn-Briley Parkway 2200 Elm Hill Pike 615/883-9770		●	●
Hyatt Regency 623 Union St. 615/259-1234	●	●	●
Marriott Hotel 1 Marriott Dr. 615/889-9300	●	●	●
Sheraton Music City 777 Mc Gavock Pike 615/885-2200	●	●	●

New Orleans, LA

Hotel	Work-out	Jogging	Swimming
Avenue Plaza 2111 St. Charles Ave. 504/566-1212	●		●
Fairmount University Place and Baronne 504/529-7111	●		●
Hilton Riverside 2 Poydras St. 504/561-0500	●	●	●
Holiday Inn Airport 2929 Williams Blvd. (Kenner) 504/467-5611	●	●	●
Holiday Inn-Crowne Plaza 333 Poydras St. 504/525-9444	●		●
Hyatt Regency Poydras Plaza at Loyola Ave. 504/561-1234		●	●
Inter-Continental 444 St. Charles St. 504/525-5566	●	●	

HOTEL

Hotel	Work-out	Jogging	Swimming
Marriott 555 Canan St. 504/581-1000	●	●	●
Meridien 614 Canal St. 504/525-6500	●		●
Royal Orleans 6121 St. Louis St. 504/529-5333	●		●
Sheraton Inn (Metairie) 3838 N. Causeway Blvd. 504/885-4890	●		●
Windsor Court 300 Gravier St. 504/523-6000	●		●

New York, NY

Hotel	Work-out	Jogging	Swimming
Golden Tulip Barbizon 140 E. 61st St. 212/838-5900	●		
Loews Summit 569 Lexington Ave. at E. 51st St. 212/752-7000	●		
Marriott-LaGuardia 102-05 Ditmars Blvd. 718/565-8900			●
Maxim's Hotel 700 Fifth Avenue 212/247-2200	●	●	●
Parker Meridien Hotel 118 W. 57th St. 212/245-5000	●	●	●
Sheraton City Squire 790 7th Ave. 212/581-3300	●		●

HOTEL

Hotel	Work-out	Jogging	Swimming
United Nations Plaza 1 United Nations Plaza 212/355-3400	●	●	●
Vista International 3 World Trade Center 212/938-9100	●	●	●

Oklahoma City, OK

Hotel	Work-out	Jogging	Swimming
Hilton Inn Airport West 401 S. Meridian 405/947-7681	●	●	●
Marriott 3233 NW Expressway 405/842-6633	●		●
Meridian Plaza 2101 S. Meridian 405/685-4000	●		●
Park Suite 1815 S. Meridian Ave. 405/682-6000	●		●
Sheraton - North 1000 E. 2nd (Edmond) 405/341-3577	●		●
Waterford 6300 Waterford Blvd. 405/848-4782	●	●	●

Orange County and South, CA
Anaheim

Hotel	Work-out	Jogging	Swimming
Disneyland 1150 W. Cerritos 714/778-6600	●	●	●
Hilton & Towers 777 Convention Way (Anaheim) 714/750-4321	●		●
Marriott 700 W. Convention Way 714/750-8000	●		●

HOTEL

Costa Mesa

Hotel	Work-out	Jogging	Swimming
Westin South Coast Plaza 666 Anton Blvd. 714/540-2500	●	●	●

Dana Point

Hotel	Work-out	Jogging	Swimming
Dana Point Resort Hotel 25135 Park Lantern 714/661-5000	●		●

Irvine

Hotel	Work-out	Jogging	Swimming
Marriott 1800 Von Karman 714/553-0100	●		●
Registry 1880 MacArthur 714/752-8777	●		●

Laguna Beach

Hotel	Work-out	Jogging	Swimming
Hotel San Maarten 696 S. Coast Hwy. 714/494-9436	●		●
Laguna Niguel The Ritz-Carlton 33533 Shoreline Dr. 714/240-2000	●	●	●

Lake Arrowhead

Hotel	Work-out	Jogging	Swimming
Arrowhead Hilton Lodge 27987 Highway 189 800/223-3307	●		●

Long Beach

Hotel	Work-out	Jogging	Swimming
Ramada Renaissance 111 Ocean Blvd. 213/437-4880	●		●

Palm Springs Area

Hotel	Work-out	Jogging	Swimming
Maxim's de Paris 285 North Palm Canyon 619/322-9000	●		●

HOTEL

Newport Beach

Hotel	Work-out	Jogging	Swimming
Four Seasons 690 Newport Dr. 714/759-0808	●		●
Marriott 900 Newport Center Dr. 714/640-4000	●		●
Hotel Meridien 4500 MacArthur 714/476-2001	●		●
The Newporter Resort 1107 Jamboree Rd 714/644-1700	●	●	●

Orange

Hotel	Work-out	Jogging	Swimming
Doubletree 100 The City Dr. 714/634-4500		●	●

San Clemente

Hotel	Work-out	Jogging	Swimming
San Clemente Inn 2600 Avenida del Presidente 714/492-6103	●		●

Orlando, FL

Hotel	Work-out	Jogging	Swimming
Contemporary Resort Box 10000 (Lake Buena Vista) 407/824-1000	●		●
Hilton at Walt Disney World Village 1751 Hotel Plaza Blvd. (Lake Buena Vista) 407/827-4000	●		●
Holiday Inn-Airport 5750 T.G. Lee Blvd. 407/851-6400	●	●	●

HOTEL

Hotel	Work-out	Jogging	Swimming
Holiday Inn-Crowne Plaza 1500 Sand Lake Rd. 407/859-1500	●		●
Marriott-Airport 7499 Augusta National Dr. 407/851-9000	●	●	●
Marriott-Orlando One World Center Dr. 407/239-4200	●	●	
Radisson Inn 8444 International Dr. 407/345-0505	●	●	●
Radisson Plaza 60 S. Ivanhoe Blvd. 407/425-4455	●	●	●
Sheraton World Int'l. Dr. & Beeline Expwy. 407/352-1100	●	●	●
Stouffer Orlando 6677 Sea Harbor Dr. 407/351-5555	●		●

Philadelphia, PA

Hotel	Work-out	Jogging	Swimming
Adam's Mark City Ave. & Monument Rd. 215/581-5000	●		●
Embassy Suites-Int'l Airport One Gateway Center 215/365-6600	●	●	●
Four Seasons One Logan Square 215/963-1500	●	●	●
Hershey Broad St. at Locust St. 215/893-1600		●	●

HOTEL	Work-out	Jogging	Swimming
Hilton-Trevose 2400 Old Lincoln Hwy. (Trevose) 215/638-8300	●	●	●
Hyatt Cherry Hill 2349 W. Marlton Pike (Cherry Hill, NJ) 609/662-3131		●	●
Marriott City Line City Line Ave. & Monument Rd. 215/667-0200		●	●
Marriott Airport 4509 Island Ave. 215/365-4150	●		●
Sheraton Society Hill One Dock St. 215/238-6000	●		●
Sheraton Valley Forge First Ave. & N. Gulph Rd. (King of Prussia) 215/337-2000	●	●	●
Warwick 17th and Locust Sts. 215/735-6000	●	●	●
Wyndam Franklin Plaza 2 Franklin Plaza 215/448-2000	●	●	●

Phoenix/Scottsdale, AZ

HOTEL	Work-out	Jogging	Swimming
Biltmore 24th St. and Missouri 602/955-6600	●	●	●
Crescent 2620 W. Dunlap Ave. 602/943-8200	●		●
Doubletree 7353 E. Indian School Rd. (Scottsdale) 602/994-9203		●	●

HOTEL	Work-out	Jogging	Swimming
Embassy Suites Tempe 4400 Rural Rd. (Tempe) 602/897-7444	●		●
Fiesta Inn 2100 Priest Dr. (Tempe) 602/967-1441	●	●	●
Hilton-Adams 111 N. Central Ave. 602/257-1525	●	●	●
Hyatt Regency 122 N. 2nd St. 602/252-1234	●	●	●
La Mancha 100 West Clarendon Ave. 602/279-9811	●		●
The Pointe 7677 N. 16th St. 602/997-2626	●	●	●
Radisson-Camelview 7601 E. Indian Bend Rd. (Scottsdale) 602/991-2400	●		●
Registry 7171 N. Scottsdale Rd. (Scottsdale) 602/991-3800	●	●	●
Sheraton Greenway Inn 2510 W. Greenway Rd. 602/993-0800		●	●
Sheraton Scottsdale 7200 N. Scottsdale Rd. (Scottsdale) 602/948-5000	●	●	●
Stouffer-Cottonwoods 6160 N. Scottsdale Rd. (Scottsdale) 602/991-1414		●	●

HOTEL

Pittsburgh, PA

Hotel	Work-out	Jogging	Swimming
Best Western Parkway 875 Greentree Rd. 412/922-7070	●		●
Harley 699 Rodi Rd. 412/244-1600	●		●
Hilton Gateway Center 412/391-4600	●		
Hyatt-Chatham Center 112 Washington Pl. 412/471-1234	●		●
Marriott-Green Tree 101 Marriott Dr. 412/922-8400	●		●
Marriott-Monroeville 101 Mall Blvd. 412/373-7300		●	●
Sheraton-Station Square 7 Station Square 412/261-2000	●		●
Sheraton Warrendale 910 Sheraton Dr., Mars US 19 412/776-6900	●		●

Portland, OR

Hotel	Work-out	Jogging	Swimming
Hilton 921 W. 6th Ave. 503/226-1611		●	●
Holiday Inn-Portland Airport 8439 NE Columbia Blvd. 503/256-5000	●	●	●
Marriott 1401 SW Front Ave. 503/226-7600	●	●	●

HOTEL

Hotel	Work-out	Jogging	Swimming
Sheraton Inn-Airport 8235 NE Airport Way 503/281-2500	●		●
Red Lion Inn Lloyd Center 1000 NE Multnomah Blvd. 503/281-6111	●		

Saint Louis, MO

Hotel	Work-out	Jogging	Swimming
Breckenridge Frontenac 1335 South Lindbergh 314/993-1100	●		●
Clarion 200 S. 4th St. 314/241-9500	●		●
Doubletree Hotel and Conference Center 16625 Swingley Ridge Rd. (Baldwin) 314/532-3000	●	●	●
Embassy Suites Downtown 901 N. 1st St. 314/241-4200	●		●
Harley 3400 Rider Trail South (Earth City) 314/291-6800	●		●
Marriott-Airport I-70 at Airport 314/423-9700	●		●
Marriott's Pavilion One Broadway 314/421-1776	●		●
Radisson 7750 Carondelet (Clayton) 314/726-5400	●		●
Radisson 9th & Convention Plaza 314/421-4000	●		●

HOTEL	Work-out	Jogging	Swimming
Sheraton 910 North 7th St. 314/231-5100	●		●
Stouffer's Concourse 9801 Natural Bridge 314/429-1100	●		●

Salt Lake City, UT

HOTEL	Work-out	Jogging	Swimming
Best Western Little America 500 S. Main St. 801/363-6781	●		●
Marriott 75 South West Temple 801/531-0800	●		●
Peery 110 W 300 S 801/521-4300	●		●
Sheraton 255 S West Temple St 801/328-2000	●		●

San Antonio, TX

HOTEL	Work-out	Jogging	Swimming
Embassy Suites 7750 Briaridge St. 512/340-5421	●		
Four Seasons 555 S. Alamo 512/229-1000	●		●
Hilton Palacio Del Rio 200 S. Alamo St. 512/222-1400	●	●	●
Holiday Inn Airport 77 N.E. Loop 410 512/349-9900	●		●
Marriott Riverwalk 711 E. Riverwalk 512/224-4555		●	●

HOTEL	Work-out	Jogging	Swimming
Sheraton North 1400 Austin Highway 512/824-5371	●		●
Wyndham 9821 Colonnade 512/691-8888	●		●

San Diego/La Jolla, CA

HOTEL	Work-out	Jogging	Swimming
Dana Inn and Marina 1710 W. Mission Bay Dr. 619/222-6440	●		●
Del Coronado 1500 Orange Ave. (Coronado) 619/435-6611	●		●
Executive 1055 1st Ave. 619/232-6141	●	●	
Hilton Beach 1775 E. Mission Bay Drive 619/276-4010	●	●	●
Holiday Inn-Embarcadero 1355 N. Harbor Dr. 619/232-3861	●		●
Humphrey's Half Moon Inn 2303 Shelter Island Dr. 619/224-3411		●	●
Intercontinental 333 W. Harbor Dr. 619/234-1500		●	●
Kona Kai 1551 Shelter Island Dr. 619/222-1191	●		
La Valencia 1132 Prospect St. (La Jolla) 619/454-0771	●		●
Mission Valley Inn 875 Hotel Circle 619/298-8281	●		●

HOTEL	Work-out	Jogging	Swimming
Plaza International 1515 Hotel Circle S. 619/291-8790	●	●	●
Sheraton Grand- Harbor Island 1590 Harbor Island Dr. 619/291-6400	●	●	●
Sheraton Harbor Island 1380 Harbor Island Dr. 619/291-2900	●	●	●

San Francisco, CA

HOTEL	Work-out	Jogging	Swimming
Clarion Hotel-Airport 401 Millbrae Ave. 415/692-6363	●		●
Fairmont Hotel 950 Mason St. 415/772-5000	●	●	
Holiday Inn Crowne Plaza 600 Airport Blvd. (Burlingame) 415/340-8500	●	●	●
Hyatt 1333 Old Bayshore Hwy. (Burlingame) 415/347-1234	●	●	●
Marriott-Airport 1800 Old Bayshore Hwy. (Burlingame) 415/692-9100	●	●	●
Ramada Renaissance Hotel 55 Cyril Magnin St. 415/392-8000	●	●	
Sheraton Inn-Airport 1177 Airport Blvd. 415/342-9200		●	●

Seattle, WA

HOTEL	Work-out	Jogging	Swimming
Doubletree Plaza 16500 Southcenter Pkwy. 206/575-8220	●	●	●
Four Seasons Olympic 411 University St. 206/621-1700	●		●
Hilton 100 112th Ave. NE (Bellevue) 206/455-3330		●	●
Holiday Inn-Crowne Plaza 6th at Seneca 206/464-1980	●		
Marriott 3201 S. 176th St. 206/241-2000	●		●
Sheraton 1400 6th Ave. 206/621-9000	●		●
Warwick 401 Lenora St. 206/443-4300	●		●
Westin 1900 5th Ave. 206/728-1000	●		●

Tampa/St. Petersburg, FL

HOTEL	Work-out	Jogging	Swimming
Admiral Benbow Inn 1200 N. Westshore Blvd. 800/237-7535	●	●	●
Guest Quarters 555 N. Westshore Blvd. 813/875-1555	●	●	●
Harbour Island Hotel 111 W. Fortune 800/HOLIDAY	●		●

HOTEL	Work-out	Jogging	Swimming
Hilton 200 Ashley Dr. at Kennedy Blvd. 813/223-2222	●	●	●
Holiday Inn Sabal Park 10315 E. Buffalo Avenue 1-800/334-6610	●	●	●
Holiday Inn - Tampa Int'l Airport 4500 W. Cypress Street. 1-800/874-8822	●	●	●
Hyatt Regency 211 N. Tampa St. 813/225-1234	●		●
Lincoln Westshore 4860 W. Kennedy Blvd. 813/873-4400		●	●
Marriott-Airport Tampa Airport 813/879-5151	●		●
Marriott Westshore 1001 N. Westshore Blvd. 813/876-9611	●		●
Sheraton Tampa East 7401 E. Hillsborough 813/626-0999	●		●

Washington, D.C.

HOTEL	Work-out	Jogging	Swimming
Grand 2350 M. St. NW 202/429-0100	●		●
Hilton 1919 Connecticut Ave. NW 202/483-3000	●	●	●
Hyatt Regency Crystal City 2799 Jefferson Davis Hwy. 703/486-1234		●	●
JW Marriott 1331 Pennsylvania Ave., NW 202/393-2000	●		●

HOTEL	Work-out	Jogging	Swimming
Loew's L'Enfant Plaza 480 L'Enfant Plaza NW 202/484-1000	●		●
Marriott Key Bridge 1401 Lee Hwy., Arlington 703/524-6400	●		●
Sheraton 2660 Woodley Rd. NW 202/328-2000	●		●
Sheraton Crystal City 1800 Jefferson Davis Hwy., Arlington 703/486-1111	●		●
Vista International 1400 "M" St., NW 202/429-1700	●	●	●
Watergate 2650 Virginia Ave., NW 202/965-2300	●	●	●
Westin 2401 M St. NW 202/429-2400	●	●	●

HOTEL

Canada

Montreal

HOTEL	Work-out	Jogging	Swimming
The Bonaventure Hilton 1 Place Bonaventure 514/878-2332 or 800/455-8667			●
Chateau Champlain 1 Place du Canada 514/878-9000 or 800/828-7477	●	●	●
Delta Montréal 450 Sherbrooke Street West 514/286-1986 or 800/268-1133	●		●
Du Parc 3625 Avenue du Parc 514/288-6666	●	●	●
Four Seasons 1050 Sherbrooke St. W. 514/284-1110	●		●
Holiday Inn Crowne Plaza 420 Sherbrooke 514/842-6111 or 800 HOLIDAY	●	●	●
La Citadelle 410 Sherbrooke 514/844-8851 or 800/361-1616	●		●
Manoir Le Moyne 2100 de Maisonneuve Blvd. 514/931-8861			
Meridian Montreal 4 Jeanne Mance Street 514/285-1450 OR 800/543-4300	●	●	●

Ottawa

HOTEL	Work-out	Jogging	Swimming
Aristocrat Apts 131 Cooper Street 613/232-9471	●	●	●
Best Western Macies 1274 Carling Avenue 613/728-1951	●		●
Cartier Place 180 Cooper Street 613/236-5000	●		●
Chateau Laurier 1 Rideau Street 613/232-6411	●		●
Delta Ottawa 361 Queen Street 613/238-6000	●	●	●
Four Seasons 150 Albert Street 613/238-1500 or 800/268-6282		●	
Holiday Inn Ottawa Centre 100 Kent 613/238-1122	●	●	●
Inn of the Provinces 360 Sparks Street 613/238-6000	●		●
The Ramada Hotel 35 Rue Laurier, Hull 613/778-6111			●
Westin 11 Colonel By Dr. 613/560-7000	●		●
Y.M. and Y.W.C.A. 180 Argyle Street 613/237-1320	●	●	●

HOTEL

Toronto

Hotel	Work-out	Jogging	Swimming
Cara Inn 6257 Airport Road 416/678-1400 or 800/387-6891	●		●
Chelsea Inn 33 Gerrard Street West 416/595-1975 or 800/268-1133	●		●
Constellation 900 Dixon Road 416/675-1500	●		●
Delta Chelsea Inn 33 Gerrard Street West 416/595-1975	●		●
Delta's Meadowvale 6750 Mississauga Road 416/821-1981	●	●	●
The Four Seasons 21 Avenue Road 416/964-0411	●	●	●
Inn on the Park 1100 Eglinton Avenue East 416/444-2561	●	●	●
Ramada Airport West 5444 Dixie Road 416/624-1144	●		●
Sheraton Centre 123 Queen Street West 800/325-3535	●	●	●
Toronto Airport Marriott 901 Dixon Road 416/674-9400	●		●
Westin Harbour Castle One Harbor Square 416/869-1600	●	●	●
Westin 145 Richmond Street 416/869-3456 or 800/228-3000	●		●

HOTEL

Vancouver

Hotel	Work-out	Jogging	Swimming
Bosman's 1060 Howe Street 604-682-3171			●
Coast Vancouver Airport 1041 S.W. Marine Drive 604/263-1555	●	●	
Delta's Airport Inn 10251 St. Edward's Drive 604/278-9611	●		●
Meridien 845 Burrard Street 604/682-5511 or 800/543-4300	●		●
Pagebrook 1234 Hornby Street 604/688-1234	●		
Pan Pacific Vancouver 999 Canada Place 604/662-8111 or 800/663-1515	●	●	
Park Royal 440 Clyde 604/926-5511			●
Relax Plaza 3071 St. Edward Drive 604/278-5155			●
Skyline Airport 3031 No. 3 Rd. 604/278-5161			●
Vancouver Mandarin 645 Howe Street 604/687-1122	●	●	●
Westin Bayshore 1601 W. Georgia Street 604/682-3377			●
Y.M.C.A. 955 Burrard Street 604/681-0221	●	●	●

United States

Albuquerque (area code 505)

Annie's Soup Kitchen
3107 Eubank
296-8601
Breakfast & Light Food - Inexpensive

Artichoke Cafe
424 Central S.E.
824-8740
American - Moderate

Cafe Oceana
1414 Central Avenue
247-2233
Seafood - Moderate

Ciao!
1550 Tramway and Indian School Road
293-2426
Northern Italian - Inexpensive

Casa Chaco
1901 University
884-2500
Continental - Moderate

Gyro's
2 locations: 106 Cornell - 255-4401
7200 Montgomery - 885-9565
Greek - Inexpensive

Knickerbockers
6601 Uptown Blvd.
883-0600
New American Cuisine - Moderate

Lo Slivale
1435 Eubank Blvd.
294-0019
Italian - Inexpensive

Luis' Place
4811 Central
255-4888
European - Moderate

Minato
10721 Montgomery & Juan Tabo
293-2929
Oriental with Sushi bar - Inexpensive

Nicole's
2101 Louisiana Blvd.
881-6800
Continental - Moderate

Nob Hill Cafe
Nob Hill Shopping Center
255-1792
Southwest American - Moderate

Oasis
5412 San Mateo
884-2324
Middle Eastern - Inexpensive

Sara's
3109 Central Avenue
256-7272
Vegetarian and fish - Moderate

Scalo
3500 Central
255-8781
Northern Italian - Inexpensive

Santa Fe (area code 505)

The Compound
653 Canyon Road
982-4353
Continental American - Expensive

E.K. Mas
319 Guadalupe
989-7121
Seafood - Moderate

El Farol
808 Canyon Road
983-9912
Spanish Tapas - Moderate

El Nido
located in Tesuque - 5 minutes from
Santa Fe Opera
988-4340
Fresh seafood and Mexican - Moderate

*Francisco's - St. Francis Hotel
210 Don Gaspar Avenue
982-8787
Italian - Moderate
*Best for breakfast

RESTAURANTS

Santa Fe (continued)

Grant Corner Inn
122 Grant Avenue
983-6678
Breakfast - Moderate

Guadalupe Cafe
313 Guadalupe Street
982-9762
Northern New Mexico - Inexpensive

Japanese Kitchen
510 N. Guadalupe Street
988-8893
Japanese Sushi - Moderate

La Casa Sena
125 East Palace Avenue
988-9232
Mexican - Moderate

La Tertulia
416 Aqua Fria
988-2769
Southwestern - Moderate

The Old House
309 W. San Francisco
988-4455
Nouvelle American - Moderate

Old Mexico Grill
2434 Cerrilos Road
473-0338
Mexican - Inexpensive

Pinon Grill
100 Sandoval Street
988-2811
New Mexican Nouvelle Cuisine - Moderate

Rosedales
907 W. Alameda
989-7411
Fish - Moderate

Santacafe'
231 Washington Avenue
984-1788
International - Moderate

*Tecolote Cafe
1203 Cerrillos Road
988-1362
Breakfast - Inexpensive
*Excellent Blueberry Pancakes

Tomasita's
500 S. Guadalupe Street
983-5721
Mexican - Inexpensive

Victor's Restorante
423 W. San Francisco Street
982-1552
Italian - Moderate

NOTE: We are particularly fond of Santa Fe. You may have already guessed this by the number of restaurants we have listed in a city of some 50,000. We intend to spend even more time suffering on your behalf to find new and deliciously healthy places for you in Santa Fe.

One of the tourist's favorites, The Coyote Cafe, has been deleted from our original list because we have been repeatedly disappointed there. It is alright for a look and a drink as long as you steer clear of their specialty, the "Watermelon Daiquiri."

RESTAURANTS

Atlanta (area code 404)

Boston Sea Party
3820 Rosewell Road
233-1776
Seafood - Moderate

Brass Key
2355 Peachtree - Peachtree Battle
Shopping Center
233-3202
Continental - Moderate

Bugatti
Omni Hotel Marietta & International Blvd.
659-0000
Northern Italian - Moderate

Capriccio
3018 Maple Drive
237-2941
Italian - Moderate

Carbo's Cafe
3717 Rosewell Road
231-4433
Continental - Expensive

Coach and Six
1776 Peachtree
872-6666
English Cuisine - Moderate

Embers
234 Hildenbrand
256-0977
Seafood - Moderate

The Fish Market Restaurant
3393 Peachtree - Lenox Square
262-3165
Seafood - Moderate

La Grotta Restorante Italiano
2637 Peachtree Road
231-1368
Northern Italian - Moderate

The Mansion
179 Ponce de Leon Avenue
876-0727
American - Moderate

Marr's Seafood Grill
1782 Cheshire Bridge Road
874-7347
Seafood - Moderate

McKinnon's Seafood Grill
3209 Maple Drive
237-1313
Seafood - Moderate

103 West Restaurant
103 West Paces Ferry Road
233-5993
Continental - Expensive

Pano and Pauls
1232 West Paces Ferry Road
261-3662
Continental - Expensive

The Restaurant
181 Peachtree - Ritz Carlton Hotel
659-0400
Continental - Expensive

Savannah Fish Company
Peachtree & International Blvd.
589-7456
Seafood - Moderate

Trotters Restaurant
3215 Peachtree Road
237-5988
American - Moderate

RESTAURANTS

Baltimore (area code 301)

The Brass Elephant
924 North Charles Street
547-8480
Continental - Expensive

Capriccio
242 South High St.
685-2710
Continental - Moderate

Danny's
1201 N. Charles
539-1393
French, American - Expensive

Ehwa
412 N. Howard Street
752-1/44
Korean, Japanese - Moderate

Gianni's Harborplace
201 E. Pratt Street #108
837-1130
Italian, Seafood - Moderate

Haussner's
3242 Eastern Avenue
327-8365
German - Inexpensive

Ikaros
4805 Eastern Avenue
633-3750
Greek - Inexpensive

Kawasaki
413 N. Charles Street
659-7600
Japanese, Seafood - Moderate

Lloyd's Cafe
925 W. Berry
332-0233
American - Inexpensive

Marconi's
106 W. Saratoga Street
727-9522
French, Italian - Moderate

Obrycki's
1729 East Pratt Street
732-6399
Seafood - Inexpensive

Phillips Harborplace
Light Street Pavilion
685-6600
Seafood - Moderate

Rio Lisboa
4700 Eastern Avenue
522-5092
Portugese, Brazilian - Moderate

Shogun
316 N. Charles Street
962-1130
Japanese, Sushi bar - Moderate

Sisson's
36 East Cross Street
539-2093
Cajun Creole - Moderate

Tandoor
Pratt Street Pavilion
547-0575
Indian - Inexpensive

Taverna Athena
Pratt Street Pavilion
547-8900
Greek - Moderate

Velleggia's
204 S. High Street
685-2620
Italian - Moderate

Wharf - Ocean City
12801 N. Coastal Highway
524-1001
Seafood - Moderate

RESTAURANTS

Boston (area code 617)

Anthony's Pier 4
140 Northern Avenue
423-6363
Seafood - Moderate

Averof - Cambridge
1924 Massachusetts Avenue
354-4500
Greek - Moderate

Cafe Budapest
90 Exeter Street
266-1979
Central European - Moderate

Davio's and Davio's Cafe
269 Newberry Street
262-4810
Italian - Moderate

Devon on the Common
150 Boylston
482-0722
Electic - Expensive

Felicia's
145 A. Richmond Street
523-9885
Italian - Inexpensive

Genji
327 Newbury Street
267-5656
Japanese with Sushi - Inexpensive

Hampshire House
84 Beacon Street
227-9600
Continental - Moderate

Harvard Book Store Café
190 Newbury Street
536-0095
European, Mediterranean - Moderate

L'Espalier
30 Gloucester Street
262-3023
French Nouvelle - Expensive

Le Marquis - Lafayette Hotel
1 Avenue de Lafayette
451-2600
French - Expensive

Legal Sea Foods - Park Plaza Hotel
64 Arlington Street
426-4444
Seafood - Moderate

Marliave Restaurant
10 Bosworth Street
423-6340
Italian - Moderate

Panache - Cambridge
798 Main Street
492-9500
Continental - Moderate

Restaurant Jasper
240 Commercial Street
523-1126
Nouvelle American - Expensive

Ritz Carlton Dining Room -
Ritz Carlton Hotel
15 Arlington Street
536-5700
French - Expensive

Seasons - Bostonian Hotel
Faneuil Hall Market Place
523-3600
American - Expensive

Tigerlilies
23 Joy Street
523-0609
Nouvelle American - Moderate

Union Oyster House
41 Union Street
227-2750
American - Moderate

Villa Francesca
150 Richmond
367-2948
Italian - Moderate

RESTAURANTS

Chicago (area code 312)

Ambria
2300 North Lincoln Park West
472-5959
Nouvelle Cuisine - Moderate

Avanzare
161 E. Huron
337-8056
Northern Italian - Moderate

Cafe' Provencal
1625 Hinman - Evanston
475-2233
French - Expensive

Cape Cod Room - Drake Hotel
140 E. Walton
787-2200
Seafood - Moderate

Carlos'
429 Temple - Highland Park
432-0770
Nouvelle Cuisine - Expensive

Chestnut Street Grill
Water Tower Place
875 N. Michigan
280-2720
Seafood - Moderate

The Courtyards of Plaka
340 S. Halsted
263-0767
Greek - Inexpensive

The Dining Room - Ritz Carlton Hotel
Water Tower Place
160 E. Pearson
266-1000
French - Expensive

*Edwardo's All Natural
4001 West Devon Avenue
736-8000
Whole Wheat Vegetarian - Moderate
*Many locations

Foley's
211 E. Ohio
645-1261
American - Moderate

Froggy's
306 N. Green Bay - Highwood
433-7080
French - Inexpensive

Gordon
500 N. Clark
467-9780
American - Moderate

Jackie's
2478 N. Lincoln
880-0003
Nouvelle Cuisine - Moderate

Jimmy's Place
3420 N. Elston
539-2999
French - Expensive

La Tour - Park Hyatt Hotel
800 N. Michigan
280-2230
French Nouvelle Cuisine - Expensive

Maple Tree Inn
10730 Western
239-3688
Cajun/Creole - Moderate

N.E.W. Cuisine
360 W. Erie
642-8885
Nouvelle Cuisine - Inexpensive

Nick's Fishmarket
Monroe at Dearborn
621-0200
Seafood - Expensive

Printer's Row
550 S. Dearborn
461-0780
American - Moderate

Scoozi
410 W. Huron
943-5900
Italian - Inexpensive

Shaw's Crab House
21 E. Hubbard
527-2722
Seafood - Moderate

RESTAURANTS

Chicago (continued)

Spiaggia
980 N. Michigan
280-2750
Northern Italian - Expensive

Yoshi's Cafe
3257 N. Halsted
248-6160
Nouvelle Cuisine - Moderate

Cincinnati (area code 513)

Bon Temps
1049 Gregory St.
621-1112
Nouvelle - Moderate

The Bistro
713 Vine St.
421-8305
American, Cajun - Moderate

Charley's Crab
97768 Montgomery Road
891-7000
Seafood - Moderate

Chester's Road House
9678 Montgomery Road
793-8700
American - Moderate

Delmonico's - Westin Hotel
Fountain Square
621-7700
Seafood - Moderate

Gourmet - Terrace Hilton
15 W. 6 Street
381-4000
French - Expensive

Grand Finale
3 E. Sharon Avenue
771-5925
American - Moderate

Heritage
7664 Wooster Pike
561-9300
American - Moderate

Jay's Seafood
244 Madison Rd.
871-2888
Seafood - Moderate

*Maisonette
114 E. 6 Street
721-2260
French - Expensive
*Excellent dietary menu —
Just what we are looking for.

Orchids at Palm Court
Netherlands Plaza Hotel
35 W. 5th St.
421-1772
Continental - Expensive

Scotti's
919 Vine Street
721-9484
Italian - Moderate

Sovereign
820 Matson
471-2250
American - Moderate

RESTAURANTS

Cleveland (area code 216)

Baricelli Inn
2203 Cornell Road
791-6500
Italian - Expensive

The Commons Tap
1114 Chester Avenue
771-1010
American Cuisine - Moderate

The Dock
11706 Clifton Blvd.
221-4388
Seafood - Moderate

Don's Pomeroy House
13664 Pearl Road
572-1111
Fish - Inexpensive

French Connection
24 Public Square
696-5600
Continental - Expensive

Heck's Cafe Rocky River
19300 Detroit Road
356-2559
Cajun - Moderate

Italian Cafe
20153 Van Aken Blvd.
752-9994
Italian - Inexpensive

Pearl of the Orient
20121 Van Aken Blvd.
751-8181
Szechuan Chinese - Moderate

Pier W.
12700 Lake Avenue
228-2250
Seafood - Moderate

Ristorante Giovanni
25550 Chagrin Blvd.
831-8625
Northern Italian - Expensive

Sammy's
1400 West Tenth Street
523-5560
Seafood - Expensive

Sweetwater Cafe
1320 Huron Road
781-1150
California Cuisine - Inexpensive

That Place on Bellflower
11401 Bellflower Road
231-4469
American - Moderate

Top of the Town
100 Erieview Plaza
771-1600
Continental with low calorie desserts -
Moderate

Z Contemporary Cuisine
20600 Chagrin Blvd.
991-1580
Contemporary Cuisine - Expensive

RESTAURANTS

Dallas (area code 214)

Actuelle
2800 Routh Street
855-0440
American - Expensive

Alessio's
4117 Lomo Alto
521-3585
Italian - Moderate

Baby Routh
2708 Routh Street
871-2345
American - Moderate

Bluebonnet Cafe
2218 Greenville
828-0052
Natural - Inexpensive

Cafe Margaux
3710 Rawlins
520-1985
Cajun - Moderate

Cafe Pacific
Highland Park Village, Suite 24
526-1170
Seafood - Expensive

Celebration
4503 W. Lovers Lane
351-5681
Vegetarian - Moderate

City Cafe
5757 W. Lovers Lane
351-2233
American - Moderate

Chez Gerard
4444 McKinney
522-6865
French - Moderate

Deep Ellum Cafe
2704 Elm St.
741-9012
Contemporary - Moderate

Dream Cafe
2800 Routh Street
954-0486
American - Inexpensive

The Grape
2808 Greenville
828-1981
Continental - Moderate

Hampton's
Berkshire Court - Preston Center
739-3474
Seafood - Moderate

Javier's
4912 Cole Avenue
521-4211
Gourmet Mexican - Moderate

The Juice Bar
Crescent Spa
Four Hundred Crescent Court
871-3232
Health Bar - Inexpensive

Little Gus
1916 Greenville Avenue
826-4910
Greek - Inexpensive

Mansion on Turtle Creek
2821 Turtle Creek
526-2121
American - Expensive

Massimo Da Milano - 2 locations
    5519 Lovers Lane - 351-1426
    The Quadrangle - 871-1900
Italian - Inexpensive

Nana Grill - Loew's Anatole Hotel
2201 Stemmons Freeway
748-1200
Southwestern - Moderate

Newport's
703 McKinney
954-0220
Seafood - Expensive

Riviera
7709 Inwood
351-0094
Italian - Expensive

Dallas (continued)

Routh Street Cafe
3005 Routh
871-7161
Southwest - Expensive

Royal Tokyo
7525 Greenville
368-3304
Japanese Sushi - Moderate

Ruggeri's
2911 Routh Street
871-7377
Northern Italian - Moderate

Saigon
1731 Greenville
828-9795
Vietnamese - Inexpensive

San Simeon
2515 McKinney
871-7373
American - Expensive

Sfuzzi
2504 McKinney
871-2606
Italian - Moderate

Sushi on McKinney
4500 McKinney
521-0969
Japanese - Moderate

Thai Soon
2018 Greenville
821-7666
Vegetarian Thai - Inexpensive

Lombardi's: 2 locations
311 Market - 747-0322
4514 Travis Walk - 521-1480
Italian - Moderate

Zodiac
Neiman Marcus
1714 Main
741-6911
Lunch - Moderate

AUTHORS' NOTE: Dallas is our home and we have both lived here all our lives. We were here when "Southwestern Cuisine" was a roasted armadillo and a six-pack, so we are justifiably proud of our city's progress.

RESTAURANTS

Denver (area code 303)

Al Fresco
1523 Market Street
534-0404
Italian - Inexpensive

Athenian Restaurant
5501 E. Colfax Ave.
329-8466
Greek - Moderate

The Bay Wolf
231 Milwaukee Street
388-9221
New American Cuisine - Moderate

Cafe Giovanni
1515 Market Street
825-6555
Continental - Expensive

Cajun's Wharf
2430 S. Havana Street
671-5111
Seafood - Moderate

Campari's - Sheraton Hotel
4900 DTC Parkway
779-8899
Northern Italian - Expensive

Con Amore
1635 Clay St.
892-6673
Italian - Inexpensive

Firefly Cafe
5410 E. Colfax
388-8429
Southwestern - Inexpensive

Harvest
430 S. Colorado Blvd.
399-6652
American - Moderate

Imperial Chinese Seafood
One Broadway
698-2800
Chinese - Moderate

Plaza Cafe
1881 Curtis St.
297-8888
Seafood - Inexpensive

Pour La France
730 S. University Blvd.
744-1888
French - Inexpensive

Rattlesnake Grill
901 Larimer Street
573-8900
Southwestern - Inexpensive

The Sage Restaurant - Oxford Hotel
1600 17th Street
628-5533
New American Cuisine - Expensive

Tante Louise
4900 East Colfax
355-4488
French - Moderate

RESTAURANTS

Detroit (area code 313)

Aldo's
19143 Kelly
839-2180
Northern Italian - Expensive

The Bagley Cafe
3354 Bagley
842-1880
Turkish - Inexpensive

Cadieux Cafe
4300 Cadieux
882-8560
Seafood - Inexpensive

Cafe Creole Orleans Cuisine
1538 Franklin
259-4411
Creole - Moderate

Chez Raphael
27000 E. Sheraton Drive
348-5555
French - Expensive

The Clarkston Cafe
18 S. Main
625-5660
American - Moderate

Giovanni's
330 S. Oakwood
841-0122
Northern Italian - Moderate

Golden Mushroom
18100 W. 10 Mile Road - Southfield
559-4230
Continental - Expensive

Harlequin Cafe
8047 Agnes
331-0922
Eclectic - Moderate

The London Chop House
155 W. Congress
962-0277
Continental - Expensive

The Money Tree
333 W. Fort at Washington
961-2445
Nouvelle Cuisine - Expensive

Joe Muer's
2000 Gratiot
567-1088
Seafood - Expensive

Nippon Kai
511 W. 14 Mile
288-3210
Japanese - Moderate

Pegasus Taverna
558 Monroe
964-6800
Greek - Inexpensive

The Rhinoceros
265 Riopelle
259-2208
Continental - Moderate

The Sheik
316 E. Lafayette
964-8441
Middle East - Moderate

333 East - Omni Hotel
333 East Jefferson
222-7404
American Cuisine - Expensive

Tokyo Sushi Iwa
22601 Allen Road
676-4711
Japanese - Moderate

Vannelli
630 Woodward
961-2444
Continental - Moderate

The Whitney
4421 Woodward
832-5700
American cuisine - Expensive

RESTAURANTS

Honolulu (area code 808)

Bagwells - Hyatt Regency
2424 Kalakawa
922-9292
French - Expensive

Bon Appetit Restaurant
1778 Moava Blvd.
942-3837
French - Moderate

Byron II
1259 Ala Mona Center
949-8855
Seafood - Expensive

Canlis Restaurant
2100 Kala Kana Avenue
923-2324
American - Expensive

Che Pasta
3571 Waialae Avenue
735-1777
Italian - Moderate

Guiltless Gourmet
1489 Kapiolani Blvd.
955-6144
International - Inexpensive

Healthy's Natural Fast Foods
2525 South King Street
955-2479
Fast Food - Inexpensive

John Dominis
43 Ahui Street
523-0955
Seafood - Expensive

Keo's Thai Cuisine
625 Kapahulu Avenue
737-8240
Thai - Moderate

Nick's Fishmarket
2070 Kalakaua Avenue
955-6333
Seafood - Expensive

Ryan's Parkplace
1200 Ala Moana Blvd.
523-9132
Casual American - Inexpensive

Sergio's
445 Nohonani Street
926-3388
Italian - Expensive

Trattoria
2168 Kalia Road
923-8415
Italian - Moderate

Willows
901 Hausten Street
946-4808
Continental - Moderate

Restaurant Suntory
Kalakaua Avenue - Royal Hawaiian
Shopping Center
922-5511
Japanese - Moderate

RESTAURANTS

Houston (area code 713)

Anthony's
4611 Montrose
524-1922
Italian - Expensive

Blue Moon
1010 Banks
523-3773
American - Moderate

Cafe Annie
5860 Westheimer
780-1522
European - Expensive

Captain Benny's Half Shell
7409 Main
795-9051
Seafood - Inexpensive

Charley's 517
517 Louisiana
224-4438
American - Expensive

Chez Eddy
6560 Fannin
790-6474
Gourmet Health Cuisine - Expensive

Damian's
3011 Smith
522-0439
Italian - Moderate

India's
5704 Richmond
266-0131
Indian - Moderate

La Reserve - Inn on the Park
4 Riverway
871-8177
Continental - Expensive

Ouisie's
1708 Sunset
528-2264
Lite Cuisine - Moderate

Rao's
3700 Richmond
622-8245
Italian - Moderate

Remington Hotel
1919 Briar Oaks Lane
840-7621
Continental - Expensive

Ruggles Grill
903 Westheimer
524-3839
Southwestern - Moderate

*Tony's
1801 Post Oak Blvd.
622-6778
Italian - Expensive

Uncle Tai's
1980 Post Oak Blvd.
960-8000
Chinese - Expensive

*Tony's sent us their cookbook and we have tried several offerings-- we think they are marvelous.

RESTAURANTS

Indianapolis (area code 317)

AMICI
351-0141
5730 Brookville Road

Bombay Bicycle Club
9111 Michigan Road
872-3446
American - Moderate

C. J. Caryl's
307 E. McGalliard - Muncie
747-1125
Healthy Fast Food - Inexpensive

Daruma
3508 W. 86th Street
875-9727
Japanese - Moderate

Fletchers Grill
107 South Pennsylvania Street
632-2500
Eclectic Nouvelle American - Expensive

Garden on the Green
1200 W. 38th Street
(Indianapolis Museum of Art)
926-2628
American - Inexpensive

Glass Chimney
12901 N. Meridian Street
844-0921
Continental - Expensive

Greco's
3849 Georgetown Road
299-5533
Greek - Moderate

Joey's
249 S. Meridian Street
639-6369
North Italian - Moderate

Keystone Grill
8650 Keystone
848-5202
Seafood - Moderate

Key West Shrimp House
2861 Madison Avenue
787-5353
Seafood - Moderate

Majectic Oyster Bar and Grill
47 South Pennsylvania Street
636-5418
Seafood - Moderate

Maxi
36 South Pennsylvania Street
631-6294
Northern Italian - Expensive

The Marker - Adams Mark Hotel
2544 Executive Drive
248-8182
American - Moderate

Parthenon
6319 N. Grilford
251-3138
Greek - Moderate

Still Water
929 E. Westfield Blvd.
259-1921
Healthfood - Moderate

Waterson's-Raddison Hotel
8787 Keystone Crossing
846-2700
Casual American - Moderate

RESTAURANTS

Jacksonville (area code 904)

Admiralty - Sheraton Hotel
1515 Prudential Drive
396-5100
French - Expensive

Crawdaddy's
1643 Prudential Drive
396-3546
Cajun, Creole - Moderate

Crustaceans Restaurant
2321 Beach Blvd.
241-8238
American - Inexpensive

The Hilltop Club
2030 Wells Road
272-5959
Seafood - Moderate

Jackie's Seafood Kitchen
531 Trout River Drive
764-0120
Seafood - Moderate

Kaldi's
4201 St. John Avenue
387-2270
Seafood - Moderate

Patti's Italian & American Restaurant
7300 Beach Blvd.
725-1662
Italian - Inexpensive

Kansas City (area code 816)

The American
Grand and 25th Street
471-8050
American - Moderate

Bristol Bar and Grill
4740 Jefferson
756-0606
Seafood - Moderate

Cafe Allegro
1815 West 39th Street
561-3663
American - Moderate

Fedora Cafe
210 West 47th Street
561-6565
Continental - Moderate

Jaspers
405 West 75th Street
363-3003
Italian - Expensive

La Bonne Auberge
725 Main Street
474-7025
French - Moderate

Pam Pam West Coffee Shop -
Alameda Plaza Hotel
Wornall Road at Ward Parkway
756-1500
American - Moderate

The Prospect of Westport
4109 Pennsylvania Avenue
753-2227

Lakeside Restaurant - Park Place Hotel
1601 N. University Avenue
483-9900
Lite American - Inexpensive

Savoy Grill
9th and Central Streets
842-3890
American - Expensive

Three Compasses
66 Cowcross St.
253-3368
American - Moderate

RESTAURANTS

Las Vegas (area code 702)

Andre's
401 South Sixth Street
385-5016
French - Expensive

Battista's Hole in the Wall
4041 Audrie
732-1424
Italian - Moderate

Bootlegger
5025 Eastern Avenue
736-4939
Italian - Moderate

Cafe Michelle
Mission Shopping Center
735-8686
Greek - Moderate

Ginza Restaurant
1000 East Sahara Avenue
732-3080
Japanese, Sushi bar - Moderate

Liberace's Tivoli Gardens
1775 East Tropicana Avenue
739-8762
Continental - Expensive

Pamplemousse
400 East Sahara Avenue
733-2066
French - Expensive

Spanish Steps - Caesar's Palace
3570 Las Vegas Boulevard
731-7560
Spanish - Expensive

State Street
2570 State Street
733-0225
Italian - Moderate

The Swiss Cafe
1431 East Charleston Blvd.
382-6444
Swiss - Moderate

(There are relatively few restaurants (or people) outside the many hotels in Las Vegas. Every large hotel has a variety of restaurants and you should be able to find a number serving healthy foods.)

RESTAURANTS

Los Angeles (area code 213)

Adriano's Ristorante
2930 Beverly Glen Circle
475-9807
Italian - Moderate

Bel-Air Hotel
701 Stone Canyon Road
472-1211
Nouvelle California - Expensive

Berty's
11712 San Vicente Blvd.
207-6169
Nouvelle - Moderate

Chan Dara
1511 N. Cahuenga Boulevard
464-8585
Thai - Moderate

Chaya Brasserie
8741 Alden Lane
859-8833
Italian, Japanese - Moderate

Chinois on Main
2709 Main Street
392-9025
French-Chinese Cuisine - Expensive

Dragon Regency
120 S. Atlantic Boulevard - Monterey
 Park
818/282-1089
Chinese - Moderate

400 N. Canon
400 N. Canon Dr.
271-1856
California Cuisine - Moderate

Fresco
415 S. Brand Blvd. - Glendale
818/247-5541
Northern Italian - Moderate

Golden Wok Seafood
13211 South St. Cerritos
860-1672
Chinese - Inexpensive

La Bruschetta
1621 Westwood Blvd.
477-1052
Northern Italian - Moderate

La Petite Chaya
1930 Hillhurst Avenue
665-5991
French, Japanese - Expensive

La Scala Malibu
3835 S. Cross Creek Road
456-1979
Italian - Moderate

Michael's
1147 Third Street
451-0843
Nouvelle California - Expensive

Nowhere Cafe
8009 Beverly Blvd.
655-8895
Natural - Moderate

Ocean Avenue Seafood
1401 Ocean Avenue
394-5669
Fish - Moderate

Orleans
11705 National Blvd.
479-4187
Cajun, Creole - Moderate

Parkway Grill
510 S. Arroyo Parkway - Pasadena
818/795-1001
Nouvelle California - Moderate

Prego
362 N. Camden Drive
277-7346
Italian - Moderate

Saigon Flavor
1044 Fairfax Avenue
935-1564
Vietnamese - Inexpensive

Saint Estéphe
2640 N. Sepulveda Blvd.
545-1334
Southwest Cuisine - Expensive

RESTAURANTS

Los Angeles (continued)

Siamese Princess
8048 W. Third Street
653-2643
Thai - Moderate

Spago
1114 Horn Avenue
652-4025
Nouvelle Californian - Expensive

385 North
385 N. La Cienega Blvd.
657-3850
California Cuisine - Expensive

Trattori Angeli
11651 Santa Monica Blvd.
478-1191
Italian - Moderate

(It is obvious that these restaurants are spread out all over the area. There are few "downtown," but that is true of the hotels as well.)

RESTAURANTS

Louisville (area code 502)

Bristol Bar & Grille
5 Riverfront Plaza
583-3342
International Cuisine - Moderate

Butterfields
4001 Dupont Circle
895-3548
American - Inexpensive

Casa Grisanti
1000 E. Liberty
584-4377
Northern Italian - Expensive

Emperor of China Restaurant
210 Holiday Manor
426-1717
Chinese - Moderate

Equus
122 Sears Avenue
897-9721
Seafood - Expensive

Ferd Grisanti's Restaurant
10212 Taylorsville Road
267-0090
Italian - Moderate

La Peche
1147 Bardstown Road
451-0377
American - Inexpensive

L. & N. Seafood Grill
303 N. Hurstbourne Lane
425-8558
American - Moderate

Masterson's Food and Drink
1830 S. Third Street
636-2511
Greek - Moderate

Sixth Avenue
600 W. Main Steet
587-6664
American - Moderate

RESTAURANTS

Memphis (area code 901)

Bayou Bar & Grill
2101 Overton Square Lane
278-8626
Cajun - Moderate

Cafe Meridien
680 Adams
525-1170
American - Expensive

Chez Philippe - Peabody Hotel
149 Union Avenue
529-4188
Nouvelle French - Expensive

Dux - Peabody Hotel
149 Union Avenue
529-4199
Seafood - Expensive

Edo
4792 Summer
767-7096
Japanese - Moderate

Giovanni's
282 North Cleveland
725-6660
Italian - Moderate

The Iris Room - Holiday Inn
Poplar at I-240
682-7881
California Cuisine - Moderate

Jim's Place East
5560 Shelby Oaks Drive
388-7200
Greek - Moderate

L. & N. Seafood Grill
1251 Park Place Center
683-3985
Seafood - Moderate

La Montagne
3550 Park
458-1060
Natural Cuisine - Moderate

Lotus
4970 Summer
682-1151
Vietnamese - Moderate

The Market Place
7722 Poplar
754-5800
Seafood - Moderate

Palm Court
2101 Overton Square Lane
725-6797
Northern Italian - Expensive

Riverside Grill
1 Beale Street
525-1116
American - Moderate

Ronnie Grisanti and Son's
162 Beale Street
527-7668
Italian - Moderate

Sakura
3121 South Mendenhall
366-4990
Japanese - Moderate

The Unicorn
6655 Poplar
754-0170
Greek - Moderate

Wah Nam
4375 Stage Road
388-8430
Chinese - Moderate

RESTAURANTS

Miami (area code 305)

Andrew's Riverside - Ft. Lauderdale
Two South River Drive West
763-7911
Seafood - Moderate

Arturo's Ristorante
6750 N. Federal Hwy.
997-7373
Italian - Expensive

The Big Splash - Kendall
8727 S. Dixie Hwy.
665-0044
Seafood - Moderate

Cafe Chauveron - Bar Harbour
9561 E. Bay Harbor Dr.
866-8779
French - Expensive

Cafe Max - Pompano Beach
2601 E. Attanlic Blvd.
782-0606
California Cuisine - Moderate

Capriccio
12312 S. Dixie Kendall
255-3422
Italian - Moderate

Chez Allen
19088 N.E. 29 Avenue
935-2900
New American Cuisine - Expensive

D'Andrea's
8745 Sunset Drive
271-4745
Northern Italian - Moderate

The Down Under - Ft. Lauderdale
3000 E. Oakland Park Blvd.
563-4123
French - Expensive

Epicurean - Palm Beach
3315 County Road
659-2005
New Continental Cuisine - Expensive

Fisherman's Warf - Boward
222 Pompano Beach Blvd.
941-5522
Seafood - Moderate

The Grand Cafe' - Grand Bay Hotel -
Coconut Grove
2669 S. Bayshore Drive
858-9600
Continental - Expensive

Granny Feelgoods
1905 E. 1st Avenue
358-6233
Natural - Moderate

Great American Cafe
5050 Town Ctr. Circle
395-3300
American - Moderate

Islas Canarias - Little Havana
287 N.W. 27th Avenue
554-7633
Latin - Inexpensive

Joe's Seafood Restaurant
400 N.W. North River Dr.
374-5637
Seafood - Moderate

Joe's Stone Crab
227 Biscayne Street
673-0365
Seafood - Moderate

Leo's Salty Sea
1136 E. Hillsboro Blvd.
421-3932
Seafood - Inexpensive

Nobi - Ft. Lauderdale
3020 N. Federal Hwy.
561-3686
Japanese - Moderate

Siam Lotus Room - S. Miami
6388 S. Dixie Hwy.
666-8134
Thai - Inexpensive

Thai Orchid
9565 S. W. 72nd
279-8585
Thai - Moderate

Toshi - S. Miami
5759 S.W. 40th Street
661-0511
Japanese, Sushi Bar - Moderate

RESTAURANTS

Milwaukee (area code 414)

And Tony's
2000 S. 8th Street
643-0077
Northern Italian - Moderate

Cafe La Boheme
319 E. Mason Street
224-0150
Greek - Moderate

Chip and Py's
815 5th Street
645-3435
American - Moderate

Coffee Trader
2625 N. Downer Avenue
332-9690
Eclectic - Inexpensive

The English Room
424 E. Wisconsin Avenue
273-8222
French - Expensive

Fountain Blue Restaurant
5133 S. Lake Drive
481-8222
Polish - Moderate

George Pandl's in Bayside
8825 N. Lake Drive
352-1430
American - Moderate

Giovanni's
1638 N. Van Buren Street
291-5600
Italian - Moderate

Inn of the Four Seasons
Highways 99 and E in Eagle
594-3318
Italian - Moderate

Jeff Toy's Sun Garden
770 N. Jefferson Street
271-1211
Chinese - Inexpensive

John Byron's
777 E. Wisconsin Avenue
291-5220
French American - Expensive

John Ernst Cafe
600 E. Ogden
273-1878
German - Moderate

Khyber Restaurant
770 N. Jefferson Street
277-7777
East Indian - Moderate

Le Bistro
509 W. Wisconsin - Marc Plaza Hotel
271-7250
French - Expensive

Mader's
1037 N. 3rd Street
271-3377
German - Moderate

Miss Katie's Diner
1900 W. Claybourn
344-0044
American - Inexpensive

Pasta Tree
1503 N. Farwell Avenue
276-8867
Italian - Moderate

Steven Wade's Cafe - New Berlin
17001 W. Greenfield Avenue
787-0774
Seafood - Expensive

West Bank Cafe
732 E. Burleigh Street
562-5555
Vegetarian - Moderate

RESTAURANTS

Minneapolis/St. Paul
(area code 612)

Minneapolis

Alison's
3008 Hennepin Avenue South
827-2816
American - Inexpensive

Aurora - Bloomington
I-494 and Highway 100
835-7800
Regional American - Expensive

Cafe Brenda
300 1st Avenue
342-9230
American - Moderate

Ciattis Italian Ristorante
1346 La Salle Avenue South
339-7747
Italian - Inexpensive

Delites of India
1123 Lake Street West
823-2866
Indian - Inexpensive

510 Restaurant
510 Groveland Avenue
874-6440
Nouvelle French - Expensive

Leeann Chin Chinese - Minnetonka
1571 Plymouth Road South
545-3600
Chinese - Moderate

Lucia's
1432 W. 31st
825-1572
Continental - Moderate

New French Café
128 N. 4th
338-3790
Nouvelle French - Expensive

Primavera
275 Market
339-8000
American Nouvelle - Moderate

Pronto Ristorante
1300 Nicollet Mall
333-4414
Northern Italian - Expensive

Sri Lanka Curry House
2821 Hennepin Avenue South
871-2400
Sri Lankan - Moderate

Sorrel's Marriott Hotel - Bloomington
1919 E. 78th Street
854-7441
Northern Italian - Expensive

Toza/Teppanyaki Room - Quality Inn
I-494 and Highway 55
553-1600
Japanese - Expensive

Trovaré
1 E. Little Canada Road
483-1805
Nouvelle American - Moderate

The Willows - Hyatt Regency Hotel
1300 Nicollet Mall
370-1234
Nouvelle American - Expensive

Yvette
65 Main Street Southeast
379-1111
Continental - Moderate

St. Paul

Blue Horse - W. St. Paul
1355 University Avenue
645-8101
Continental - Expensive

Cafe Latté
850 Grand Avenue
224-5687
American - Inexpensive

Caravan Serai - St. Paul
2046 Pinehurst Avenue
690-1935
Middle Eastern - Moderate

RESTAURANTS

St. Paul (continued)

Nashville (area code 615)

Fuji-ya
420 1st
339-2226
Japanese, Sushi Bar - Expensive

It's Greek to Me
626 Lake Street West
825-9922
Greek - Inexpensive

Koglak's Royal Oak
4785 Hodgson Road
484-8484
American - Moderate

L'etoile
St. Paul Hotel
292-9292
Continental - Moderate

Lexington
1096 Grand Avenue
222-5878
American - Expensive

The New Lido Italian Ristorante -
Roseville
2801 Snelling Avenue North
636-9721
Italian - Moderate

Saji-ya on Grand
695 Grand Avenue
292-0444
Japanese - Moderate

Arthur's
Mall at Green Hills
383-8841
Continental - Expensive

Belair - Sheraton Music City Hotel
777 McGavock Pk.
885-2200
American - Moderate

Benkay
40 White Bridge Road
356-6600
Japanese Sushi Bar - Moderate

Broadway's Union Station Hotel
1001 Broadway
726-1001
Seafood - Expensive

Brother's Ristorante
1907 West End Avenue
327-0148
Italian - Moderate

Christopher's Belle Meade Plaza
Harding Road
383-5900
Continental - Expensive

Ciraco's Italian Cuisine
212 1st Avenue
329-0036
Italian - Moderate

Crawdaddy's
14 Oldham Street
255-5434
Seafood - Expensive

The Crown Court Maxwell House Hotel
2025 Metrocenter Blvd.
259-4343
New American - Moderate

Jullan's Restaurant Francais
2412 West End Avenue
327-2412
French - Expensive

RESTAURANTS

Nashville (continued)

KaTo
212 Fourth Avenue S.
255-8122
Japanese, Sushi Bar - Moderate

L & N Seafood Grill
2817 West End Avenue
327-9610
Seafood - Moderate

Niko's
102 19th Avenue S.
329-0004
Greek - Moderate

Tran's
71 Hermitage Avenue
726-2921
Vietnamese - Inexpensive

Upper Crust
2120 West End Avenue
329-2244
Continental - Expensive

New Orleans (area code 504)

Antoine's
713 St. Louis Street
581-4422
French Creole - Expensive

Bon Ton Cafe
401 Magazine Street
524-3386
Cajun - Moderate

Caribbean Room - Pontchartran Hotel
2031 St. Charles Avenue
524-0581
French, Creole Cuisine - Expensive

Casemento's
4330 Magazine Street
895-9761
Italian, Seafood - Moderate

*Commander's Palace
1403 Washington Avenue
899-8221
French Creole - Expensive

Felix's
739 Iberville
522-1440
Oyster Bar - Moderate

Indulgence
1501 Washington Avenue
899-4411
"Lite" Cuisine - Moderate

K-Paul's Louisiana Kitchen
416 Chartres Street
942-7500
Hot! Cajun - Moderate

Sazerac Restaurant - Fairmont Hotel
University Place
529-7111
Continental - Expensive

Upperline
1413 Upperline
891-9822
Seafood - Moderate

*In addition to being at the top of New Orleans dining, Commander's features "Lite dishes" as well. We found this an exceptional restaurant.
New Orleans is a city full of wonderful restaurants serving marvelous seafood, but beware of the rich creamy sauces and, oh, those desserts!

RESTAURANTS

New York (area code 212)

*We can chew our way across Manhattan
and clearly see our middles fatten
The variety in New York City
Leaves us sitting pretty
So many restaurants to treasure
That one must carefully measure
The ingredients for a start
To hang on to a healthy heart!*

Anatolia
1422 Third Avenue
517-6262
Turkish - Moderate

Arcadia
21 E. 62nd Street
223-2900
Nouvelle American - Expensive

Arizona 206
206 E. 60th Street
838-0440
Southwestern - Expensive

Awoki
305 E. 46th Street
759-8897
Japanese - Moderate

Barbetta
321 W. 46th
246-9171
Italian - Expensive

Bravo Gianni
230 East 63rd Street
752-7272
Italian - Moderate

Brive
405 East 58th Street
838-9393
French - Expensive

Cafe Greco
1390 Second Avenue
737-4300
Mediterranean - Moderate

Chez Louis
1016 Second Avenue
752-1400
French - Expensive

China Grill
60 West 53rd Street
333-7788
French/Chinese - Expensive

David K's
1115 Third Avenue
371-9091
Chinese - Moderate

Felidia
243 E 58th Street
758-1479
Northern Italian - Moderate

Four Seasons
99 E. 52nd Street
754-9494
International - Expensive

Gianni's
15 Fulton Street
608-7300
Northern Italian - Moderate

Gotham Bar & Grill
12 E. 12th Street
620-4020
Italian - Expensive

Il Monello
1460 Second Avenue at 76th Street
535-9310
Italian - Moderate

Il Nido
251 E. 53 Street
753-8450
Italian - Moderate

Indian Oven I
285 Columbus Avenue
362-7567
2nd Location: 913 Broadway
460-5744
Indian - Moderate

La Colombe d'Or
134 E. 26th Street
689-0666
French - Moderate

145

RESTAURANTS

New York (continued)

Le Bernardin
155 W. 51st
489-1515
Seafood - Expensive

Le Cirque
58 E. 65th
794-9292
French - Expensive

Manhattan Ocean Club
57 W. 58th Street
371-7777
Seafood - Expensive

Marylou's
21 W. 9th Street
533-0012
Seafood - Moderate

Mitusukoshi
461 Park Avenue
935-6444
Japanese - Expensive

Nanni's
146 E. 64th
599-9684
Northern Italian - Expensive

Oriental Town Seafood
14 Elizabeth Street
619-0085
Chinese - Moderate

Oyster Bar and Restaurant
Grand Central Terminal
490-6650
Seafood - Moderate

Palio
151 W. 51st
245-4850
Italian - Expensive

Provence
38 MacDougal Street
475-7500
French - Expensive

Rakel
231 Varick Street
929-1630
Seafood - Expensive

Savant
132 Lexington Avenue
686-3959
Healthy Cuisine - Moderate

Shun Lee Palace
155 East 55th Street
371-8844
Chinese - Moderate

Sweet Victory Cafe
1157 Third Avenue
570-1620
Low Calorie Natural - Inexpensive

Texarkana
64 West 10th Street
254-5800
American - Moderate

Toscana Ristorante
246 E. 54th
371-8144
Italian - Expensive

Zarela
2nd Avenue between 50 & 51st
644-6740
Seafood - Moderate

Zucchini
1336 First Avenue
249-0559
Vegetarian - Moderate

RESTAURANTS

Oklahoma City (area code 405)

Alberta's Tea Room
French Market Mall
842-3458
American - Moderate

Christopher's
2920 Grand Blvd.
943-8395
French - Moderate

Eagle's Nest
5900 Mosteller Drive
840-5655
Continental - Expensive

Glen's Hickory Inn
2815 N.W. 10 Street
943-4445
American - Moderate

Magnolia Cafe
6714 N. Western
848-1026
Creole - Moderate

Tony's Via Roma
2743 N.W. Hwy.
843-2462
Italian - Moderate

Orange County (area code 714)

Anaheim

Adrienne's - Sheraton - Anaheim
1015 W. Ball Road
778-1700
Nouvelle American - Moderate

The Catch Restaurant
1929 S. State College
634-1829
Seafood - Moderate

China Dynasty
1154 N. Euclid Avenue
774-8890
Chinese - Moderate

Hastings - Anaheim Hilton & Towers
777 Convention Way
750-4321
Cuisine Courant - Expensive

Luccis D'Italia
1287 E. Lincoln Avenue
533-1300
Italian - Inexpensive

Mr. Stox Restaurant
1105 E. Katella Avenue
634-2994
Seafood - Moderate

Seafood Broiler
1199 N. Euclid
788-5000
Seafood - Inexpensive

Shipyard Inn - Disneyland Hotel
1150 W. Cerritos Avenue
778-6600
Seafood - Moderate

Sushi Bar
777 Convention Way
750-4321
Japanese - Inexpensive

Orange County (continued)
Corona del Mar

Carmelo's
3520 Central Hwy.
675-1922
Italian - Moderate

Genkai
3344 E. Coast Hwy.
675-0771
Japanese - Moderate

Hemingway's Restaurant
2441 E. Coast Hwy.
673-0120
European Cuisine - Moderate

Puffin's
3050 E. Coast Hwy.
640-1573
Continental Cuisine - Moderate

Steinbecks Creatine Cuisine
217 Marine Avenue
673-0570
Continental - Moderate

Costa Mesa

Alexander's Cafe
1565 Adams
241-0123
California Cuisine - Moderate

Ango Tei
675 Paularino Avenue
557-2696
Japanese - Moderate

Copa De Oro
633 Anton Blvd.
662-2672 (662-COPA)
Nouvelle Continental - Moderate

Forty Carrots
South Coast Plaza
556-9700
Vegetarian - Moderate

Gandhi
3820 Plaza
556-7273
Indian - Moderate

Gianni
3333 Bear Street
118 Crystal Court
540-3365
Italian - Moderate

Lettuce Patch
3333 Bristol
545-8240
American - Inexpensive

McCormick's Landing
3180 Airway Avenue
546-9880
Seafood - Moderate

Ooiso Restaurant
310 E. 17th
642-0141
Japanese - Moderate

Pronto Ristorante
3333 Bristol Street
540-8038
Italian - Moderate

Rueben's
1641 W. Sunflower
979-3474
Continental - Moderate

Fullerton

Angelo's and Vinci's
516 N. Harbor Blvd.
879-4022
Italian - Moderate

The Cellar
305 N. Harbor Blvd.
525-5682
French - Expensive

Chez Panache
444 N. Harbor Blvd.
526-6633
California - Moderate

Elmer's Place
323 N. State College Blvd.
870-7400
American - Inexpensive

RESTAURANTS

Orange County (continued)

Fullerton (continued)

Mandarin Pavillion
1050 W. Valencia Drive
870-7950
Chinese - Moderate

Soup Exchange
157 E. Orangethorpe
992-5522
Soup and Salad - Inexpensive

Huntington Beach

Fu Jin
15070 Edwards Street
892-8333
Chinese - Moderate

Franco's
17041 Beach Blvd.
841-7077
Italian - Moderate

J.C. McLin's Bar & Grill
18121 Beach Blvd.
841-0417
American - Moderate

Kiku Restaurant
15059 Goldenwest
891-0401
Japanese with Sushi Bar - Inexpensive

Mama Rose's Italian Ristorante
7320 Center Drive
895-2528
Italian - Moderate

Snapper's
18685-H Main Street
841-9911
Seafood - Moderate

Theo's Restaurant
7148 Edinger Avenue
847-8069
Greek - Inexpensive

Irvine

Chinatown Restaurant & Bar
4139 Campus Drive
833-8696
Chinese - Moderate

Jade's
18000 Von Karman Avenue
553-0100
Japanese, Thai - Moderate

Le Cafe - Hilton & Towers
1700 Jamboree Blvd.
863-3111
California - Inexpensive

The Mediterranean Room - Airporter Inn
18700 MacArthur Blvd.
833-2770
Continental - Moderate

Players
18100 Von Karman
553-8181
California Cuisine - Moderate

Prego
18420 Von Karman
553-1333
Northern Italian - Moderate

Taiko Japanese Restaurant
14775 Jeffery Road
559-7190
Japanese & Sushi Bar - Inexpensive

Laguna Beach and Laguna Niguel

The Cafe
33533 Ritz Carlton Drive
240-2000
California Cuisine - Moderate

The Club Grill and Bar - Ritz Carlton Hotel
35533 Ritz Carlton Drive
240-2000
California Cuisine - Moderate

Greeter's Corner
329 S. Coast Hwy.
494-0361
Seafood - Moderate

La Chinoise
23600 Rockfield Blvd.
830-9984
Nouvelle Chinese - Moderate

RESTAURANTS

Orange County (continued)
Laguna Beach and
Laguna Niguel (continued)

Le Gourmet
30902 Coast Hwy.
499-5383
Italian - Inexpensive

Paisans
17 Monarch Bay Plaza
240-9436
Italian - Moderate

Strictly Seafood
30001 Town Center Drive
249-8000
Seafood - Inexpensive

Tavern by the Sea
2007 S. Coast Hwy.
497-6568
California - Moderate

Towers - Surf and Sands Hotel
1555 S. Coast Hwy.
497-4477
Continental Cuisine - Inexpensive

Verdi Ristorante
14120 Culver Drive
551-2201
Italian - Moderate

Newport Beach

A La Petite Cafe
500 Newport Center Drive
760-9292
Continental - Inexpensive

Antoine - Hotel Meridian
4500 MacArthur
476-2001
French - Expensive

Baxter Street
4647 Mac Arthur Blvd.
756-0611
American Cuisine - Moderate

The Bistro - The Newporter Resort
1107 Jamboree Road
644-1700
Continental - Inexpensive

California Beach
3355 Via Lido
675-0575
California Cuisine - Inexpensive

The Cannery
3010 Layfayette Avenue
675-5777
Seafood - Moderate

The Crab Cooker
2200 Newport Blvd.
673-0100
Seafood - Inexpensive

Hassan's Cafe
3325 Newport Blvd.
675-4668
Lebanese Cuisine - Moderate

Newport Oyster Bar & Grill
2100 W. Oceanfront
675-9977
Seafood - Inexpensive

Royal Khyber
1000 Bristol Street
752-5200
Indian - Moderate

The Stuft Noodle
217-17 Riverside Avenue
548-7418
Northern Italian - Moderate

Villa Nova
3131 W. Coast Hwy.
642-7880
Italian - Moderate

Orange

Cafe Capri
320 E. Katella Avenue
639-5320
Continental - Moderate

Chez Cary
571 S. Main Street
542-3595
Continental - Expensive

Koisan
1132 E. Katella Avenue
639-2330
Japanese, Sushi Bar - Moderate

RESTAURANTS

Orange County (continued)

Papa Rossi Italian Cuisine
1866 N. Tustin
998-9500
Italian - Moderate

Santa Monica Seafood Company
1700 N. Main Street
921-2632
Seafood - Inexpensive

Tandoor Cuisine of India
1132 E. Katella Avenue
538-2234
Indian - Moderate

Cherry Blossom Restaurant
3700 W. Warner Avenue
557-2074
Japanese, Sushi Bar - Moderate

Courthouse Restaurant
2 Hutton Centre Drive
545-1776
Regional American - Moderate

Horikawa
3800 S. Plaza Drive
557-2531
Japanese - Moderate

San Clemente

Andreino's
1925 S. El Camino Real
492-9955
Italian - Moderate

Bombay Cafe
35 Calle de Industrias
498-5000
Continental - Moderate

Cafe Del Coyote
301 N. El Camino Real
498-6241
Gourmet Mexican - Moderate

Swallow's San Clemente Inn
2600 Del Presidente
492-6103
American - Moderate

San Pedro

Nizetich's
1050 Nagoya Street
514-3878
Continental - Expensive

Santa Ana

Antonello Ristorante
3300 S. Plaza Drive
751-7153
Italian - Moderate

RESTAURANTS

Orlando (area code 407)

Atlantis - Wyndham Hotel
6677 Sea Harbor Drive
351-5555
Continental - Moderate

Bay Street
6115 Westwood Drive
352-2322
Seafood - Moderate

Cascades - Grand Cypress Hotel
exit 27 off I-4
239-1234
American - Moderate

Cazha
7511 International
352-3811
Greek - Moderate

Christini's Ristorante Italiano
7600 Doctor Phillips Blvd.
345-8770
Italian - Moderate

Dabar
7600 Doctor Phillips Blvd.
345-8128
Indian - Moderate

The Enclave Beach Cafe
6165 Carrier Drive
352-5740
Seafood - Moderate

Jordan's Grove - Maitland
1300 S. Orlando Avenue
628-0020
American - Moderate

Kum Tao
500 N. Orlando
740-5450
Chinese - Moderate

Mikado Japanese Restaurant
World Center Drive (I-4 exit 26A)
239-4200
Japanese - Moderate

Royal Orleans Restaurant
8445 International Drive
352-8200
American - Moderate

Seagrille
5905 Kirkman Road
345-0373

Straub's Fine Seafood: 2 locations
512 E. Altamonte Dr. - 831-2250
5101 E. Colonial Dr. - 273-9330
Seafood - Inexpensive

Thorndikes Restaurant - Radisson Plaza
60 S. Ivanhoe Blvd.
425-4455
Florida Cuisine - Expensive

J. B. Winberie - Longwood
1869 Hwy.
332-8555
American - Inexpensive

(There are numerous "fast-food" and somewhat slower restaurants in Walt Disney's World and Epcot Center.)

RESTAURANTS

Philadelphia (area code 215)

Alfredo The Original of Rome
21 S 5th Street
627-4600
Italian - Moderate

Apropos
211 S. Broad Street
546-4424
Eclectic - Moderate

Bookbinders Old Original
125 Walnut Street
925-7027
Seafood - Expensive

Cafe Nola
328 South Street
627-2950
Cajun, Creole - Moderate

The Commissary
1710 Sansom St.
569-2240
American - Moderate

D' Medici's
824 S 8th Street
922-3986
Italian - Moderate

Di Lullo Centro
1407 Locust Street
546-2000
Seafood, Pasta - Expensive

Dinardo's Famous Crabs
312 Race Street
925-5151
Seafood - Moderate

Élan - Warwick Hotel
1701 Locust Street
546-8800
Continental, Italian - Expensive

The Fountain Restaurant
Four Seasons Hotel
1 Logan Square
963-1500
Continental - Expensive

Frog
1524 Locust Street
735-8882
Continental - Expensive

Harry's Bar & Grill
22 South 18th Street
561-5757
Italian, American - Moderate

Harvest
19th & Market Street
568-6767
American - Inexpensive

Le Bec Fin
1523 Walnut Street
567-1000
French - Expensive

Morgan's Restaurant
135 South 24 Street
567-6066
Northern Italian - Expensive

October
26 South Front Street
925-4447
American - Expensive

Osteria Romana
935 Ellsworth
271-9191
Italian - Expensive

Siva's Restaurant
34 South Front Street
925-2700
Indian - Moderate

Tokio
124 Lombard St.
922-3948
Japanese - Moderate

The 20th Street Cafe
261 South 20th Street
546-6867
American - Moderate

U.S.A. Cafe at The Commissary
1710 Sansom Street
569-2240
American Southwest - Inexpensive

Wildflowers
514 South Fifth Street
923-6708
French - Moderate

RESTAURANTS

Phoenix (area code 602)

Avanti
2728 E. Thomas Road
956-0900
Continental - Expensive

Beside The Point
7677 North 16th Street
997-2626
American - Moderate

Etienne's Differt Point of View
1111 N. Seventh Street
866-7500
French - Expensive

Fish Market
1720 E. Camelback Road
277-3474
Seafood - Moderate

Greekfest
1219 E. Glendale Avenue
265-2990
Greek - Moderate

Ianuzzi Point of View
7677 N. 16th Street
997-5859
Italian - Expensive

Livia's
4221 N. Seventh Avenue
266-7144
Italian - Moderate

Orangerie - Arizona Biltmore
Missouri at 24th
954-2507
Continental - Expensive

Osome
619 W. Osborn Road
264-6578
Japanese - Moderate

Pasta Sergio's
1904 E. Camelback Road
274-2195
Italian - Moderate

Tuptim
3409 W. Thunderbird Road
863-1000
Thai - Inexpensive

Vincent on Camelback
3930 E. Camelback Road
224-0225
French - Expensive

Scottsdale (area code 602)

Ambrosino's
2122 N. Scottsdale Road
994-8404
Italian - Moderate

American Grill
6113 N. Scottsdale
948-9907
American - Moderate

Bouchon
5401 N. Scottsdale Road
947-5400
American - Expensive

Famous Pacific Fish Company
4321 N. Scottsdale Road
941-0602
Seafood - Moderate

Golden Swan - Hyatt Regency Hotel
7500 E. Doubletree Road
991-3388
American - Expensive

Mancuso's
6166 N. Scottsdale Road
948-9998
Continental - Expensive

The Market - Citadel
8700 E. Pinnacle Road
585-0635
Southwestern - Moderate

Petit Cafe
7340 E. Shoeman Lane
947-5288
French - Expensive

Shogun
12615 N. Tatum Blvd.
953-3264
Japanese - Inexpensive

Touch of Spice
13831 N. 32nd Street
992-5220
Continental - Inexpensive

RESTAURANTS

Pittsburgh (area code 412)

Angel's Corner
Atwood and Bates Streets
682-1879
American Cuisine - Moderate

Cafe Allegro
51st S. 12th
481-7788
Italian, French - Moderate

Cafe Del Sol
2104 Murray Avenue
422-1303
Spanish - Inexpensive

Carmassis
1101 Perry Highway
364-5101
Italian - Moderate

Common Plea Restaurant
308 Ross Street
281-5140
Continental - Moderate

De Nunzio's
700 Lowry Avenue
527-5552
Seafood, Pastas - Moderate

Froggy's
100 Market Street
471-3764
Seafood - Moderate

Grand Concourse
One Station Square
261-1717
Seafood - Moderate

Kiku
Station Square
765-3200
Japanese - Moderate

La Normande
5030 Centre Avenue
621-0744
French - Expensive

Le Mont
1114 Grandview Avenue
431-3100
Continental - Expensive

Shajor
422 McMurray Road
833-4800
Seafood - Moderate

RESTAURANTS

Portland (area code 503)

Atwater's - Bancorp Tower
1111 S.W. Fifth
220-3600
American - Expensive

Bush Garden
900 Southwest Morrison Street
226-7187
Japanese - Moderate

Cascades
333 N.W. 23rd Avenue
274-2305
Spa Cuisine - Expensive

Christopher's
688 Forest Avenue
772-6877
Greek - Moderate

Genoa
2832 S.E. Belmont
238-1464
Northern Italian - Expensive

Hamilton's Indian Restaurant
43 Middle Street
773-4498
Indian - Moderate

Heathman Restaurant and Bar
S.W. Broadway
241-4100
Northwest Cuisine - Expensive

J's Oyster Bar
5 Portland Pier
772-4828
Seafood - Moderate

Jack's Famous Crawfish
401 S.W. 12th
226-1419
Seafood - Moderate

Koji Osakaya
7007 S.W. Macadam
293-1066
Japanese, Sushi Bar - Moderate

Modern Times
53 N.W. First
223-0743
French - Moderate

Raphael's
36 Market Street
773-4500
Italian - Moderate

Restaurant Sapporo
24 Free Street
772-1234
Japanese, Sushi Bar - Moderate

Trojan Horse Restaurant
675 Congress Street
772-9530
Greek - Moderate

Winterborne
3520 N.E. 42nd
249-8486
Seafood - Expensive

RESTAURANTS

St. Louis (area code 314)

Agostino's Colosseum
12949 Olive Blvd.
434-2959
Italian - Moderate

Al Baker's
8101 Clayton Road
863-8878
Continental - Moderate

American Rotisserie Restaurant & Bar
Omni International Hotel
#1 St. Louis Union Station
241-3636
Nouvelle American - Expensive

Bar Italia
4656 Maryland
361-7010
Italian Nouvelle - Inexpensive

Bernard's Bar & Bistro
26 N. Meramic
727-7004
French - Inexpensive

Cafe Marrakesh
1740 S. Brentwood Blvd.
962-0333
Spanish Tapas - Moderate

Gian Peppe's
2126 Marconi
772-3303
Italian - Moderate

Giovanni's
5201 Shaw
772-5958
Italian - Moderate

Greek Gourmet
721 New Ballas
569-1001
Greek - Inexpensive

Redel's
310 De Baliviere
367-7005
Nouvelle American - Moderate

Richard Perry
3265 S. Jefferson Avenue
771-4100
Nouvelle American - Moderate

S. & P. Oyster Company
14501 Manchester Road
256-3300
Seafood - Inexpensive

2nd Street Diner
721 N. 2nd Street
436-2222
Seafood - Inexpensive

Spiro's
3122 Watson Road
645-8383
Greek - Moderate

Tony's
826 N. Broadway
231-7007
Italian - Moderate

RESTAURANTS

Salt Lake City (area code 801)

American Grill
4835 Highland Drive
277-7082
American - Moderate

Asakusa Sushi
321 S. Main
364-7142
Sushi - Moderate

Bird's Cafe
1355 East 2100 South
466-1051
California Cuisine - Moderate

Brumby's
224 South 1300 East
583-0469
Contemporary - Moderate

Cafe Central
104 Trolley Square
531-0895
American - Moderate

Cafe Pierpont
126 W. Pierpont
364-1222
Mexican - Moderate

Charlie Chow
Trolley Square
575-6700
Thai - Inexpensive

Crompton's Roadside Attraction
5195 Emigration
583-1869
American - Moderate

Erik's
10263 So. 1300 E. Sandy
572-6123
Continental - Expensive

Ferrantelli
300 Trolley Square
531-8228
Italian - Moderate

Kyoto
1300 S. 1080 E.
487-3525
Japanese - Moderate

Liaison Restaurant
1352 South 2100 East
583-8144
French - Moderate

The Long Life Vegi House
1353 E. 3300 So.
467-1111
Vegetarian - Moderate

Market Street Broiler
260 S. 1300 E.
583-8808
Seafood - Moderate

Mikado
67 West 100th South
328-0929
Japanese - Moderate

The Other Place Restaurant
473 E. 300 South
521-6567
Greek - Inexpensive

Pasta Mulino
859 East 900 South
364-8066
Italian - Inexpensive

Shenanigan's Restaurant
274 S. W. Temple
364-3663
American - Moderate

RESTAURANTS

San Antonio (area code 512)

Al-Arz Restaurant
5137 Fredericksburg
344-2212
Oriental - Moderate

Aldo's Ristorante Italiano
8539 Fredireksburg
696-2536 (696-ALDO)
Italian - Expensive

Anaqua Room - Four Seasons Hotel
555 Alamo
229-1000
Southwest Cuisine

The Bayous
517 N. Presa
223-6403
Cajun - Moderate

Cappy's
5011 Broadway
828-9669
American - Moderate

Crescendo - Hyatt Regency
123 Losoya
222-1234
Seafood - Expensive

Little Italy
824 Afterglow
349-2060
Italian - Moderate

Niki's Tokyo Inn
819 W. Hildebrand
736-5471
Japanese, Sushi Bar - Moderate

Nona's Homemade Pasta
2809 N. St. Mary's
736-9896
Pastas - Moderate

P.J.'s
One Riverwalk Place
225-8400
Southwestern - Expensive

Pearl Inn
11815 IH-10 West
696-3355
Chinese - Moderate

Pelican's Landing
2525 Jackson-Keller
344-1451
Seafood - Moderate

Polo's - Fairmount Hotel
401 S. Alamo
225-4242
Southwestern Cuisine - Expensive

Shogun
421 E. Commerce
222-1112
Japanese, Sushi Bar - Moderate

Steamers Cafe
300 Bitters at West Avenue
494-1940
Southwest - Moderate

RESTAURANTS

San Diego (area code 619)

Anthony's Fish Gratto
1360 N. Harbor Drive
232-5103
Seafood - Inexpensive

Benjamin's - Solana Beach
145 S. Hwy. 101
259-0733
American Cuisine - Expensive

The Blue Crab Restaurant
4922 Harbor Drive
224-3000
Seafood - Inexpensive

Borel's
5323 Mission Center Road
295-6600
Southwestern - Moderate

Cafe Pacifica
2414 San Diego Avenue
291-6666
Seafood - Moderate

Celadon
3628 Fifth Avenue
295-8800
Asian - Inexpensive

Chateau Orleans
926 Turquoise Street
488-6744
Louisiana Style Cajun - Moderate

Dobson's
956 Broadway Circle
231-6771
International - Moderate

Di Canti Ristorante - La Jolla
5721 La Jolla Blvd.
454-1177
Italian - Moderate

Fallbrook Grocery Cafe - Fallbrook
321 E. Alvarado Street
723-0588
European Style - Moderate

George's at the Cove - La Jolla
1250 Prospect
454-4244
California Cuisine - Moderate

Greek Town
431 E. Street
232-0461
Greek - Moderate

Gustaf Anders - La Jolla
2182 Avenida de la Plaza
459-4499
Continental - Expensive

Harbor House Top of the Plaza
510 Horton Plaza
233-5923
All Types - Moderate

Jerry G. Bishops
879 W. Harbor Drive
239-5216
Fastfood Greek - Inexpensive

La Gran Tapa
611 B. Street
234-8272
Spanish Tapas - Moderate

Nino's - Pacific Beach
4501 Mission Bay Drive
274-3141
Italian - Expensive

Papagayo
861 W. Harbor Drive
232-7581
Seafood - Moderate

Sapporo
4529 Mission Bay Drive
270-1183
Japanese, Sushi Bar - Moderate

Yakitori II
3740 Sports Arena Blvd.
223-2641
Japanese, Sushi Bar - Moderate

160

RESTAURANTS

San Francisco (area code 415)

Atlantis
361 West Portal Avenue
665-7920
Seafood - Moderate

Blue Fox
659 Merchant Street
981-1177
Continental - Expensive

Cafe Riggio
4112 Geary Blvd.
221-2114
Nouvelle Cuisine - Moderate

Campton Place Restaurant
340 Stocklon Street
781-5155
American - Moderate

China Moon Cafe
639 Post
775-4789
Chinese - Moderate

Eddie Jack's
1151 Folsom Street
626-2388
Seafood - Moderate

Ernie's
847 Montgomery
397-5969
Nouvelle French - Expensive

Fior D'Italia
601 Union Street
986-1886
Italian - Moderate

Fleur de Lys
777 Shutter Street
673-7779
French - Expensive

Golden Turtle
2211 Van Ness Avenue
441-4419
Vietnamese - Moderate

Greens
Ft. Mason Building A
771-6222
Vegetarian - Moderate

Hayes Street Grill
324 Hayes Street
863-5545
Seafood - Moderate

Hillcrest Bar & Cafe
2201 Fillmore Street
563-8400
American - Moderate

Janot's
44 Campton Place
392-5373
Nouvelle Cuisine - Moderate

Kinokawa
347 Grant
398-8226
Japanese, Sushi Bar - Moderate

La Pergola: 2 locations
    2060 Chestnut St. - 563-4500
    1198 Treat Ave. - 648-2223
Italian - Expensive

Mandarin
Ghiradelli Square
673-8812
Chinese - Expensive

Modesto Lanzone's
601 Van Ness - Civic Center
928-0400
Italian - Expensive

Nakamura
209 Pier 39
421-6818
Japanese - Moderate

Pasha
1516 Broadway
885-4477
Morroccan - Moderate

RESTAURANTS

San Francisco (continued)

Raffles Restaurant
1390 Market Street
621-8601
Polynesian Chinese - Moderate

Scoma's Fishermans Wharf
Pier 47
771-4383
Seafood - Expensive

Scott's Seafood Bar & Grill
2400 Lombardi Street
563-8988
Seafood - Moderate

Silks - The Mandarin Oriental
222 Sansome Street
986-2020
French, Oriental - Moderate

Stars
555 Golden Gate
861-7827
California Cuisine - Expensive

Berkeley (area code 415)

Chez Pannisse
1517 Shattuck Avenue
548-5525
Nouvelle Cuisine - Expensive

Fourth Street Grill
1820 Fourth Street
849-0526
Italian - Moderate

Santa Fe Bar & Grill
1310 University Avenue
841-4740
Southwest - Moderate

Salomon Grundy's
100 Seawall Drive
548-1876
American Seafood - Moderate

Spenger's Fish Grotto
1919 Fourth Street
845-7771
Seafood - Inexpensive

RESTAURANTS

Seattle (area code 206)

Alexis Restaurant
1007 First Avenue
624-4844
French - Expensive

Benjamin's
10655 N.E. Fourth
454-8255
Continental - Moderate

Canlis Restaurant
2576 Aurora Avenue North
283-3313
American - Expensive

Fullers - Sheraton Hotel
Sixth & Union
621-9000
Northwest - Expensive

Gravity Bar
86 Pine
443-9694
Health Foods - Inexpensive

Il Bistro
93 A - Pike Street
682-3049
West Coast Italian - Expensive

Il Terrazzo
411 First Avenue S
467-7797
Italian - Moderate

Ivar's Indian Salmon House
401 N.E. Northlake Way
632-0767
American - Moderate

Le Provencal Restaurant Francais
212 Central
827-3300
French - Moderate

Nikko Restaurant
1306 S. King Street
322-4641
Japanese, Sushi Bar - Moderate

The Oyster Bar
240 Chucknut Drive
766-6185
Seafood - Expensive

Prego - Stouffer Madison Hotel
515 Madison Street
583-0300
Northern Italian - Moderate

Rosellini's Four-10
2515 Fourth Avenue
728-0410
Continental - Expensive

Rosellini's Other Place
319 Union Street
623-7340
French - Expensive

The Shoalwater Restaurant -
Shelburne Inn
Hwy. 103 and N. 45th Seaview
642-4142
Regional Cuisine - Expensive

Umberto
100 S. King Street
621-0575
Northern Italian - Moderate

Union Bay Cafe
3505 N.E. 45th
527-8364
Mediterranean - Moderate

Taps at Green Lake
7200 Green Lake
522-8277
Northwest Cuisine - Moderate

RESTAURANTS

Tampa/St. Petersburg (area code 813)

Bradenton

Cia's Petite Cafe
18305 59th Street West
794-5468
American Cuisine - Moderate

High Seas Restaurant
9915 Manatee Avenue West
792-4776
Continental Cuisine - Moderate

The Pier Restaurant - Bradenton
Memorial Pier
748-8087
Seafood - Moderate

Clearwater

Bill Knapp's - Clearwater
3120 U.S. 19 North
797-8825
General Dietary - Moderate

Bombay Bicycle Club - Clearwater
2721 Gulf to Bay Blvd.
799-1841
Seafood - Moderate

Calico Jack's - Adam's Mark Hotel
430 S. Gulfview Blvd.
442-4442
Seafood - Moderate

Dolce Vita - Clearwater
2561 Countryside Blvd.
791-1552
Italian - Moderate

Heilman's Beachcomber - Clearwater
447 Mandalay Avenue
442-3151
Seafood - Moderate

Hooter's
2800 Gulf to Bay Blvd.
797-4008
Seafood - Inexpensive

Dunedin

Bon Appetit - Dunedin
150 Marina Plaza - Jamaica Inn
733-2151
European - Expensive

Chef Charley's - Dunedin
1800 Main Street
736-2502
American - Inexpensive

Oldsmar

Boston Cooker
1130 SR 584 - Forest Lakes Plaza
855-2311
Seafood - Moderate

Palmetto

Crab Trap
Terra Ceia Bridge
722-6255
Seafood - Moderate

St. Petersburg

Don CeSar
3400 Gulf Blvd.
360-1881
Seafood - Moderate

Hooters
2901 Tyrone
343-4947
Seafood - Inexpensive

Rolland & Pierre
2221 4th Street North
822-4602
French - Expensive

Sarasota

Cafe L'Europe
431 Harding Circle Street
388-4415
Continental - Expensive

The Colony
1620 Gulf of Mexico Dr - Longboat Key
383-5558
New American - Moderate

Tampa/St. Petersburg (continued)

Sarasota (continued)

Michael's on East
1212 East Avenue
366-0007
American Cuisine - Moderate

Robin and Joel's Fish Company
7500 South Tamiami Trail
922-2466
Seafood - Moderate

Windjammer - Davey's Locker
6700 South Tamiami Trail
922-1595
Seafood - Moderate

Tampa

Armani's - Hyatt Regency
6200 Courtney Campbell Causeway
874-1234
Italian - Expensive

Bella Pasta and Pizza
1413 S. Howard
254-3355
Italian - Moderate

Donatello
232 N. Dale Mabry
875-6660
Italian - Expensive

Island Room
725 S. Harbor Drive
299-5000
Continental - Expensive

Lauro Ristorante
4010 West Waters Avenue
884-4366
North Italian - Moderate

Lorenzo's
3615 W. Humphrey
932-6641
Southern Italian - Moderate

Millers Seafood Center
2315 West Linebaugh Road
935-4793
Seafood - Moderate

Salt Water Bar & Grille - Hyatt Regency
Tampa and Jackson Streets
225-1234
Seafood - Moderate

Spanish Park
3517 East 7th Avenue
248-6138
Spanish - Moderate

Sukhothai
8201 North Dale Mabry
933-7990
Oriental - Moderate

Valencia Garden
811 W. Kennedy Blvd.
253-3773
Spanish - Moderate

Tarpon Springs

Louis Pappas
10 West Dodecanese Street
813/937-5101
Greek - Moderate

RESTAURANTS

Washington, D.C. (area code 202)

Apana
3066 M. Street N.W.
965-3040
Indian - Expensive

Au Fruits de Mer
1329 Wisconsin Avenue N.W.
965-2377
Seafood - Moderate

Bacchus
1827 Jefferson Pl.
785-0734
Lebanese - Moderate

Cantina D'Italia
1214A 18th St. N.W.
659-1830
Italian - Expensive

Crisfields
8012 George Avenue
589-1306
Seafood - Expensive

Germaine's
2400 Wisconsin Avenue N.W.
965-1185
Asian - Expensive

Italian Oven
2809 M. St. N.W.
337-0730
Northern Italian - Moderate

Jean-Louis at Watergate -
Watergate Hotel
2650 Virginia Avenue, N.W.
298-4488
French - Expensive

La Brasserie
239 Massachusetts Avenue N.E.
546-6066
Nouvelle French - Moderate

La Chaumiere
2813 M. Street, N.W.
338-1784
Seafood - Moderate

Le Lion d'Or
1150 Connecticut Avenue N.W.
269-7972
French - Expensive

Market Inn
200 E. Street, S.W.
554-2100
American - Moderate

Marrakesh Restaurant
617 New York Avenue, N.W.
393-9393
North African - Moderate

Matuba
2915 Colombia Pike - Arlington
521-2811
Japanese, Sushi - Moderate

Piccolo Mondo
1835 K Street N.W.
223-6661
Italian - Moderate

Restaurant Nora
2132 Florida Avenue N.W.
462-5143
Nouvelle California - Expensive

Rossini's Ristorante D'Italia
5507 Connecticut Avenue N.W.
244-7774
Italian - Moderate

Shezan
913 19th Street N.W.
659-5555
Pakistani - Expensive

Siam Inn
11407 Amherst Avenue
942-0075
Thai - Inexpensive

Takesushi
1010 20th N.W.
466-3798
Japanese with Sushi - Moderate

209 1/2
209 1/2 Pennsylvania Avenue S.E.
544-6352
New American - Expensive

Vincenzo
1606 20th St. N.W.
667-0047
Italian, Seafood - Expensive

Windows
1000 Wilson Boulevard - Arlington
527-4430
Nouvelle California - Expensive

RESTAURANTS

Montreal, Canada
(area code 514)

Arigato
75 de la Gauchetiere Street West
395-2470
Japanese - Moderate

Cafe de Paris - Ritz Carlton
1228 Sherbrooke Street West
842-4212
French - Expensive

Casa Pedro
1471 Crescent Street
288-1314
Spanish - Moderate

Chez Delmo
211 rue Notre-Dame Ouest
849-4061
Seafood - Moderate

Chez Pauzé
1657 Ste-Catherine
932-6118
Seafood - Expensive

Desjardins
1175 Mackay
866-9741
Seafood - Expensive

Dionysus
5301 Park Avenue
277-8940
Greek - Inexpensive

La Casa Grecque
200 Prince Arthur
842-6098
Greek - Inexpensive

La Marée
404 Place Jacques - Cartier
861-8126
Fish - Expensive

La Medina
3464 St-Denis
282-0359
Moroccan - Moderate

La Pagode
138 St. Paul St. E.
861-6640
Vietnamese - Inexpensive

La Sila
2040 St. Denis
844-5083
Italian - Moderate

Le Commensal
2115 St. Denis
845-2627
Inventive Vegetarian - Inexpensive

Le Fadeau
423 St-Claude
878-3959
French - Expensive

Le Latini
1130 Jeanne Mance
861-3166
Italian - Moderate

Milos
5357 Ave. du Parc
272-3522
Greek - Moderate

Mount Everest
5160 Sherbrooke
483-1482
Nepali Cuisine - Inexpensive

Vespucci
124 Prince Arthur East
843-4784
Italian - Inexpensive

RESTAURANTS

Ottawa, Canada
(area code 613)

Brokerage (Three locations)
Place de Ville
238-5273
90 Sparks
232-6385
Rideau Centre
230-8001
Light Cuisine - Inexpensive

Cafe Henry Burger
69 Laurier, Hull
819/777-5646
French - Expensive

Clair de Lune
81 B. Clarence Street
230-0022
French - Moderate

Flippers
823 Bank Street
232-2703
Seafood - Expensive

Green Valley
1107 Prince of Wales Dr.
225-8770
French - Moderate

Haveli
87 George Street
230-3566
Indian - Moderate

Hayloft Portside
202 Rideau Street
236-6863
Seafood - Moderate

Icho
87 George Street
230-6857
Japanese - Moderate

Il Vagabondo
186 Barrette Street
749-4877
Italian - Moderate

Le Café
National Arts Center
594-5127
Light Cuisine - Moderate

Le Soupçon
408 Rideau Street
594-8808
French - Moderate

Moroccan Village (2 Locations)
77 Clarence
230-2421
1542 Bank Street
521-8964
Moroccan - Moderate

Old Fish Market
54 York Street
563-4954
Fish - Moderate

The Ritz (3 Locations)
1665 Bank
238-3270
274 Elgin
235-7027
15 Clarence
234-3499
Eclectic - Inexpensive

Savana Cafe
431 Gilmour Street
233-9159
Eclectic - Moderate

AUTHORS' NOTE: One of the delights of preparing our book was the rediscovery of the new Ottawa. We found an abundance of exercise facilities located in hotels and many health conscious restaurants. Exercising comes easy: When it is warm, walking through the beautiful downtown parks; when it is cold, skating on the Rideau Canal, which is frozen into the world's longest ice rink. Visiting the brand-new National Gallery of Canada by Montreal architect Moshe Safdie was thrilling. The difference that we found in six years was amazing. Ottawa is a Canadian treasure!

RESTAURANTS

Toronto, Canada
(area code 416)

Beaujolais
165 John Street
598-4656
Continental - Moderate

Bocca
49 St. Clair Avenue West
960-8808
Italian - Expensive

Cafe Creole - Skyline Hotel
655 Dixon Road
244-1711
American - Moderate

Centro
2472 Yonge Street
483-2211
Eclectic - Expensive

Edo
359 Eglinton Avenue West
481-1370
Japanese - Moderate

Joso's
202 Davenport Road
925-1903
Seafood - Moderate

Julien
387 King Street West
596-6738
French - Expensive

La Fenice
319 King Street West
585-2377
Italian - Moderate

La Pergola
154 Cumberland Street
922-3543
Italian - Moderate

Lee Garden
358 Spadina Avenue
593-9524
Chinese - Inexpensive

Loons
2306 Queen Street East
698-1440
Eclectic - Inexpensive

Mermaid
330 Dundas Street West
597-0077
Seafood - Modest

Pronto
692 Mount Pleasant Road
486-1111
Eclectic California - Expensive

The Puffin
150 Eglinton Avenue East
487-0487
American - Moderate

Raja Sahib
254 Adelaide Street West
593-4756
Indian - Inexpensive

Saigon Star
4 Collier Street
922-5840
Franco/Vietnamese - Moderate

Scalini
1133 Yonge Street
923-1744
Italian/French - Moderate

Simcoe
136 Simcoe Street
591-7541
Eclectic - Moderate to Expensive

Vasco da Gama
892 College St.
535-1555
Portuguese - Moderate

Zaidy's
275 Queen Street
977-7222
Cajun - Inexpensive

RESTAURANTS

Vancouver, Canada
(area code 604)

A Kettle of Fish
900 Pacific Street
682-6661
Fish - Moderate

Cafe de Medici
1025 Robson Street
669-9322
Italian - Moderate

Cannery Seafood
2205 Commissioner Street
254-9606
Seafood - Expensive

The Cristal - Mandarin Hotel
645 Howe Street
687-1122
Continental - Expensive

Danish Tea Room
1068 Robson Street
683-3732
Danish/Indian - Inexpensive

Flamingo House
7510 Cambie Street
325-4511
Chinese - Inexpensive

Hy's
1523 Davie Street
689-1111
Seafood - Moderate

Kamei Sushi (2 Locations)
   811 Thurlow Street
   684-5767
   1414 Broadway
   732-0112
Japanese - Moderate

Las Tapas
760 Cambie Street
669-1624
Spanish - Moderate

Le Pavillion - Four Seasons Hotel
791 W. Georgia Street
689-9333
French - Expensive

Little Franks
1487 Robson Street
687-7291
Italian - Moderate

Mulvaney's
1535 Johnston St - Granville Island
685-6571
Cajun/Creole - Moderate

The Noodle Makers
122 Powell Street
683-9196
Chinese - Moderate

Ostera Napoli
1660 Renfrew Street
255-6441
Italian - Moderate

Pink Pearl
1132 E. Hastings Street
253-4316
Dim sum - Inexpensive

Rooster's Quarters
836 Denman Street
689-8023
Chicken - Moderate

Saigon
1500 Robson Street
682-8020
Vietnamese - Moderate

Simpatico's
2222 West Fourth Avenue
733-6824
Greek - Moderate

The Teahouse
Ferguson Point
669-3281
Seafood - Expensive

Umberto al Porto
321 Water Street
683-8376
Italian - Moderate

The Vegetable Patch
1484 Broadway
738-5233
Salad Bar - Inexpensive

References

1. Goldman L, Cook EF. The decline in ischemic heart disease mortality rates. Ann Intern Med 1984;202:825-36.

2. Alabaster O. The power of prevention: reduce your risk of cancer through diet and nutrition. New York: Simon & Schuster, Inc., 1986.

3. Manson JE, Stampfer MJ, Hennekens CH, Willett WC. Body weight and longevity: a reassessment. JAMA 1987;257:353-8.

4. Stamler J, Liu K. The benefits of prevention. In: Kaplan NM, Stamler J, eds. Prevention of coronary heart disease. Philadelphia: WB Saunders Company, 1983:188-207.

5. Anonymous. Study finds epidemic of childhood obesity. The New York Times 1987 May 1.

6. Hall T. Americans are returning to the sweet life. The New York Times 1987 March 11.

7. Dannenberg AL, Drizd T, Horan MJ, Haynes SG, Leaverton PE. Progress in the battle against hypertension: changes in blood pressure levels in the United States from 1960 to 1980. Hypertension 1987;10:226-33.

8. Blakeslee S. Nicotine: harder to kick than heroin. The New York Times Magazine 1987 March 29.

9. Vega GL, Grundy SM. Mechanisms of primary hypercholesterolemia in humans. Am Heart J 1987;113:493-502.

10. Blankenhorn DH, Nessim SA, Johnson RL, et al. Beneficial effects of combined colestipol-niacin therapy on coronary atherosclerosis and coronary venous bypass grafts. JAMA 1987;257:3233-40.

11. Grundy SM. HMG-CoA reductase inhibitors for treatment of hypercholesterolemia. N Engl J Med 1988;319:24-33.

12. National Center for Health Statistics - National Heart, Lung, and Blood Institute Collaborative Lipid Group. Trends in serum cholesterol levels among US adults aged 20 to 74 years: data from the National Health and Nutrition Examination Surveys, 1960 to 1980. JAMA 1987;257:937-42.

13. The Expert Panel. Report of the National Cholesterol Education Program Expert Panel on detection, evaluation, and treatment of high blood cholesterol in adults. Arch Intern Med 1988;148:36-69.

14. Eaton SB, Konner M, Shostak M. Stone agers in the fast lane: chronic degenerative diseases in evolutionary perspective. Am J Med 1988;84:739-49.

15. Bonanome A, Grundy SM. Effect of dietary stearic acid on plasma cholesterol and lipoprotein levels. N Engl J Med 1988;318:1244-48.

16. McNamara DJ, Kolb R, Parker TS, et al. Heterogeneity of cholesterol homeostasis in man. J Clin Invest 1987;79:1729-39.

17. Edington J, Geekie M, Carter R, et al. Effect of dietary cholesterol on plasma cholesterol concentration in subjects following reduced fat, high fibre diet. Br Med J 1987;294:333-6.

18. Morgan BLG. The truth about fish oils. Nutr and Hlth 1987;9:1-6.

19. Grundy SM. Comparison of monounsaturated fatty acids and carbohydrates for lowering plasma cholesterol. N Engl J Med 1986; 314:745-8.

20. Mensink RP, Katan MB. Effect of monounsaturated fatty acids versus complex carbohydrates on high-density lipoproteins in healthy men and women. Lancet 1987;1:122-4.

21. McConnell C, McConnell M. The olive. In: McConnell C, McConnell M, eds. The Mediterranean diet: wine, pasta, olive oil, and a long healthy life. New York: W W Norton & Company, Inc., 1987:57-67.

22. Keys A, Menotti A, Karvonen MJ, et al. The diet and 15-year death rate in the seven countries study. Am J Epidemiol 1986;124:903-15.

23. Kleinfield NR. Across America, the fish are jumpin'. The New York Times 1987 March 1.

24. Kromhout D, Bosschieter EB, de Lezenne Coulander C. The inverse relation between fish consumption and 20-year mortality from coronary heart disease. N Engl J Med 1985;312:1205-1209.

25. Herold PM, Kinsella JE. Fish oil consumption and decreased risk of cardiovascular disease: a comparison of findings from animal and human feeding trials. Am J Clin Nutr 1986;43:566-98.

26. Kaplan NM. Treatment of hypertension: nondrug therapy and the rationale for drug therapy. In: Kaplan NM, ed. Clinical hypertension, 4th ed. Baltimore: Williams and Wilkins, 1986:147-79.

27. Donahue RP, Abbott RD, Bloom E, Reed DM, Yano K. Central obesity and coronary heart disease in men. Lancet 1987;1:821-824.

28. Hershcopf RJ, Bradlow HL. Obesity, diet, endogenous estrogens, and the risk of hormone-sensitive cancer. Am J Clin Nutr 1987;45:283-289.

29. Eastwood M. Dietary fiber and the risk of cancer. Nutrition Reviews 1987;45:193-98.

30. Birt DF. Update on the effects of vitamins A, C, and E and selenium on carcinogenesis. Proc Soc Exper Biol Med 1986;183:311-320.

31. Ames BN. Dietary carcinogens and anticarcinogens. Oxygen radicals and degenerative diseases. Science 1983;221:1256-1264.

32. Associated Press. Physician warns of a generation of fat children. The New York Times, 1987 August 27:16.

33. Reinhold R. Has the aerobics movement peaked? An interview with Kenneth Cooper. The New York Times, 1987 March 29:14,16,102.

34. Anonymous. Moderate exercise slows CAD. Medical World News 1987 August 10:26-27.

35. Paffenbarger RS Jr, Hyde TR, Wing MA. Physical activity, all-cause mortality, and longevity of college alumni. N Engl J Med 1986;314:605-13.

36. Benson H. The Relaxation Response. New York: Morrow, 1975.

37. Holmes TH, Rahe RHJ. The social readjustment rating scale. Psychosom Res 1967;11:213-18.

38. Rose G, Marmot MG. Social class and coronary heart disease. Br Heart J 1981;45:13-19.

39. Friedman M, Powell LH, Thoresen CE, et al. Effect of discontinuance of type A behavioral counseling on type A behavior and cardiac recurrence rate of post myocardial infarction patients. Am Heart J 1987;114:483.

40. Beard J. Science supports the three-hour lunch break. New Scientist 1987 February 12:33.

41. Staszewski S, Schieck E, Rehmet S, Helm EB, Stille W. HIV transmission from male after only two sexual contacts. Lancet 1987;2:628.

42. Schatzkin A, Jones Y, Hoover RN, et al. Alcohol consumption and breast cancer in the epidemiologic follow-up study of the First National Health and Nutrition Examination Survey. N Engl J Med 1987;316:1169-1173.

43. Willett WC, Stampfer MJ, Colditz GA, et al. Moderate alcohol consumption and the risk of breast cancer. N Engl J Med 1987;316:1174-80.

44. Report from FDA's Sugars Task Force, Evaluation of health aspects of sugars contained in carbohydrate sweeteners. J Nutr 1986;116:115.

45.   Blume E. Overdosing on protein. Nutrition Action 1987;14:1,40-6.

46.   Council on Scientific Affairs. Vitamin preparations as dietary supplements and as therapeutic agents. JAMA 1986;257:1929-1936.

47.   Nutrition Committee, American Heart Association. Dietary guidelines for healthy American adults. Circulation 1986;74:1465A-1468A.

48.   Steptoe A. Managing flying phobia. Br Med J 1988;296:1756-57.

49.   Harding RM, Mills FJ. Medical aspects of airline operations. II. Aircrew schedules and emergency considerations. Br Med J 1983;287:37-39.

50.   Seidel WF, Roth T, Roehrs T, Zorick F, Dement WC. Treatment of a 12-hour shift of sleep schedule with benzodiazepines. Science 1984;224:1262-1264.

51.   Mills FJ, Harding RM. Fitness to travel by air. I. Physiological considerations. Br Med J 1983;286:1269-1271.

52.   Larson EB, Roach RC, Schoene RB, Hornbein TF. Acute mountain sickness and acetazolamide. JAMA 1982;248:328-332.

53.   Rock PB, Johnson TS, Cymerman A, Burse RL, Falk LJ, Fulco CS. Effect of dexamethasone on symptoms of acute mountain sickness at Pikes Peak, Colorado (4,300 m). Aviat Space Environ Med 1987;668-672.

Order Form

If you would like to order additional copies of TRAVEL WELL, *please call:*

1-800-225-0694

or write:

Essential Medical Information Systems, Inc.
P.O. Box 811124   Dallas, TX 75381

☐ *Charge It*   ☐ Visa_____

☐ *Bill Me*   ☐ MasterCard_____

☐ *Check Enclosed*   Expiration Date_____

Please send me _____ *copy(s) of* TRAVEL WELL *at $12.95 each, plus $1.30 per book for shipping and handling.*

_____
First   Middle Initial   Last

_____
(If business address, please indicate company name here.)

_____
Street Address or P.O. Box Number

_____
City   State   Zip

_____
Telephone Number